The World's Greatest Military Spies and Secret Service Agents

The World's Greatest Military
Spies and Secret Service Agents

THE CAPTURE OF MAJOR ANDRÉ *(See page 67)*

The WORLD'S GREATEST MILITARY SPIES and
Secret Service Agents

By GEORGE BARTON

Illustrated

THE PAGE COMPANY
BOSTON ❀ PUBLISHERS

Made in U. S. A.

Third Impression, August, 1926

TO

WILLIAM J. FLYNN
CHIEF OF
THE UNITED STATES SECRET SERVICE

WHOSE UNTIRING EFFORTS
RID THIS COUNTRY OF FOREIGN SPIES
DURING THE WORLD'S GREATEST WAR

INTRODUCTION

The romance of war in its most thrilling form is exemplified in this narrative of the adventures of "The World's Greatest Military Spies and Secret Service Agents." Much has been published upon the subject of espionage, and the memoirs and secret histories of the courts of Europe give us instances of men and women who have gained favor and money, if not honor and glory, by selling back-stairs gossip concerning their fellow creatures; but the aim of the present work has been rather to relate the big exploits of those who faced great personal danger and risked their lives for the sake of flag and country.

Each story is complete in itself, and yet forms a link in the chain of narratives which illustrates the startling and unexpected manner in which battles have been lost and won through the shrewdness and the courage of military spies at various times in different countries of the world. All spies are not admirable. Indeed, some whose deeds are herein related seem despicable. The use of the word " spy " in this series is in its broadest, and usually its best, sense. In all of the great wars of history there have been spies, scouts, emissaries and others still with no very well defined status, who have rendered invaluable service to their governments. A spy is liable to death; a

viii   INTRODUCTION

scout, if captured, has the rights of a prisoner of war,
but an emissary is rather political than military, and is
sent to influence secretly the opposition rather than to
bring information concerning the movements of troops.

There are spies and spies.   Just where the line is to
be drawn must depend largely upon the personal view-
point of the reader.   Some of those who have been engaged in hazardous military exploits are looked upon
as among the world's greatest heroes; others who have
abused the hospitality of their entertainers in order
to betray them have earned never-ending obloquy.
Everything depends upon the circumstances and the
point of view.   Human nature has been the same in all
ages.   We are disposed to justify and glorify the military spy who risks his life for our own country and our
own cause, and to condemn and abuse the one who is
enlisted in the service of the enemy.

Generally speaking, there is a natural repugnance to
the professional spy in times of war, who is regarded
as akin to the paid informer in times of peace.   But
the tendency is to applaud the real soldier who is willing to depart from the strict lines of military duty
in order to serve his country.   Napoleon, who can
scarcely be called a scrupulous man, even by his most
ardent admirers, refused to bestow the medal of honor
on his chief spy.   " Money, as much as you like," he
exclaimed, " but the cross — never ! "

At the time of the capture of Emilio Aguinaldo by
the late Brigadier-General Frederick Funston a question arose regarding the ethics of the means employed
by some of the members of the troops under his com-

mand on that occasion. It arose in a lecture before the law class at the University of the Philippines. Justice Carson, of the Supreme Court, was asked to enlighten the students on this point. Instead of doing so, he wrote and asked General Funston's view of the matter. The reply of the American soldier may be accepted as the authorized military view of the question. General Funston wrote:

" In a nutshell, the legal status of all those engaged in the expedition referred to was that of spies, and as such they could not have claimed immunity from the usual fate of spies. While we were not disguised for the purpose of obtaining information, the fact that we penetrated the enemy's lines under false colors would have justified treating us as such.

" Having acknowledged that our status was that of spies, I wish to call attention to a popular, erroneous belief that spies are violators of the laws of war simply because they are spies and in disguise. It is safe to say that there never has been a war in which both sides did not use spies; in fact, the principal military nations use them in time of peace. Spies are punished, not because there is anything morally reprehensible in their work, but because it is desired to make their occupations so dangerous that it will be difficult to find men to undertake the risks involved.

" The status of the spy in our own history cannot better be shown than in the fact that Nathan Hale, the spy of our own Revolution, whose impressive statue stands in New York and whose last words on the gallows were: ' My chief regret is that I have but one

life to give for my country,' is one of the greatest of
our national heroes.

"Washington has been regarded always as one of
the most scrupulous of men, but he did not hesitate to
hold as a prisoner the British general Prescott, captured by Colonel Barton of the Rhode Island militia
and a few men, all disguised as non-combatants, who
penetrated the British lines under false colors.

"Although the use of spies is not a violation of
the laws of war, there are certain acts that are recognized as such and may be punished by death: The
violation of the flag of truce; breaking a truce; violation of parole; the use of poison; killing of prisoners
of war to prevent their recapture, and hoisting the hospital flag over a place not a hospital. But all these
imply moral obliquity, and I have never heard of any
one being rewarded or having a monument erected to
him for having been guilty of any one of them.

"The Filipinos are about the last people in the world
who can question the ethics of entering the enemy's
lines in disguise. As a veteran of the war you know
that, disguised as non-combatants, their officers and
soldiers are among us all the time, and that if we had
enforced the law strictly relative to spies we would
have been hanging men all the time."

The halo of romance hovers in a special manner over
women spies, and it is interesting to note that the
United States furnishes the most conspicuous exam-
ples of this class in the persons of Belle Boyd, the Confederate girl who saved Stonewall Jackson; and Emma
Edmonds, the Union spy, whose adventures could

scarcely be duplicated in the pages of fiction. The story of a third American woman is related in this volume — Lydia Darrah, the gentle and brave Quakeress who saved Washington's army from destruction. She was not a spy in the accepted sense of the word, and it would be impossible to imagine a greater contrast than is presented between the colonial girl and the two women of the Civil War, but the service she rendered the young and struggling nation cannot be overestimated.

A book of this character would not be complete without the stories of Nathan Hale and Major André, the American and the Briton, each young and gallant, and each giving up his life for his country. In a general way, their exploits are familiar, yet it may be found that a new light has been turned upon certain phases of the sacrifices which they both so cheerfully made for the causes they represented.

An effort has been made to confine this work to the operations of military spies, but in possibly two instances the rule has been relaxed in order to present phases of that form of diplomacy which is so closely allied with war as to be part of it. Most of the incidents are interwoven with the history of the countries to which they relate, and are part of the archives of the State, War and Navy Departments of these nations. Taken all in all, the pages of fiction contain few things more fascinating or thrilling than these fact stories.

G. B.

CONTENTS

CONTENTS

LIST OF ILLUSTRATIONS

I

THE ALSATIAN SMUGGLER WHO HELPED
NAPOLEON TO CAPTURE THE
AUSTRIAN ARMY

The World's Greatest Military Spies and Secret Service Agents

I

THE ALSATIAN SMUGGLER WHO HELPED NAPOLEON TO CAPTURE THE AUSTRIAN ARMY

THIS is the story of a thrilling episode in the life of a man who has been called the Prince of Spies. His name was Charles Louis Schulmeister and he played a most invaluable part in building the fame of no less a person than Napoleon Bonaparte. What the greatest military genius of his time might have accomplished without the aid of his wonderfully effective secret service system must be left to the imagination. What he actually did with the assistance of Charles Louis Schulmeister and his associates is one of the most fascinating parts of the secret archives of France and Austria.

First a word concerning the life and personality of this famous military spy. He was a native of an Alsatian village — New Freistell in the Grand Duchy of Baden, on the right bank of the Rhine. He was an adventurous boy and his early life was filled with hair-raising escapades. It was the most natural thing in the world for such a youth to develop into a smuggler and for years he followed that calling to the dismay of the authorities and to the advantage of his personal fortunes.

Schulmeister was of medium build, brusque in his manner and movements, smooth-faced and with two ugly scars on his forehead, the result of bravery in battle. He had blue eyes, clear, penetrating and unwavering. He was quick to think and prompt to execute; shrewd, smart and full of courage and resolution. Also, Schulmeister was absolutely devoid of the sense of fear.

In 1805 Napoleon was at Strassburg planning his wonderful Austrian campaign. His camp at Boulogne was marvelous and its size calculated to strike terror into the heart of the enemy. But the Corsican did not propose to move until he was fully informed of the extent and character of the forces he would be called upon to meet. He wanted a shrewd and tried man in the camp of the enemy. In this emergency he sent for General Savery, the head of the French Secret Service, and informed him of his desire. The officer saluted.

"Sire, I have the very man you need for this mission."

Savery, who was not particularly noted for his scrupulousness, had a score of fearless men at his beck and call, and not the least of them was Charles Louis Schulmeister. The Alsatian smuggler had been on Savery's staff for years, and had performed delicate missions with great success. The moment Napoleon spoke Savery decided to employ Schulmeister for this latest dangerous mission. He had the young Alsatian brought to him and informed him of the Emperor's wishes.

"The Emperor wishes to see you personally and at once," he said.

Schulmeister was skeptical. He rubbed his brawny hand across the scars on his forehead:

"You are having sport with me."

"Not at all," was the vehement rejoinder. "The Emperor wishes to see you on a matter of great importance. Be prepared to meet him at any moment."

The Alsatian sat down and awaited the summons, but not without some trepidation. He recalled the lawless career he had pursued, prior to his military service, and he wondered if he was called to give an account of his misdeeds. Yet the Great Man of Destiny would scarcely waste his time on such secondary and trivial matters. Possibly he had been misrepresented to the Emperor. In that event he would truly have reason to shake in his boots, for Napoleon made short shrift of those whose loyalty was not absolutely unquestioned.

But with that phase of the business Schulmeister straightened out his shoulders and was filled with resolution. He knew that he had been faithful to Napoleon and France; whatever other defects there might be in his character — and they were many and serious — disloyalty was not one of them. As to meeting the great man — pshaw! that was but part of the day's work.

" Schulmeister, come forward! "

This command from an officer awakened the young Alsatian from his day dreams. He was being conducted to the presence of the man whose name was already reverberating around the world. He followed closely on the heels of the messenger, wondering why he had been summoned and how he should act. Before he could map out any coherent line of conduct he realized that he was in the headquarters of the Emperor.

Schulmeister looked about him quickly and for the moment was confused. The place was filled with staff officers wearing glittering uniforms and talking in low but animated tones. Which of these could be the Emperor? He looked for the most impressive uniform but was not enlightened. Presently his glance fell upon a man short in stature, but well formed and resolute in his manner. He was apart from the others and restlessly paced up and down the narrow limits of the apartment. He wore a long gray coat over a plain uniform. He turned around unexpectedly and moved out of the mass of gorgeously uniformed men. The Alsatian recognized him at once.

It was Napoleon.

At first the Emperor's smooth face, firmly set jaw and rigid mouth seemed to portend a storm. But as his eyes rested on the young man he smiled charmingly and engagingly. The glance that he shot at his visitor was at once ardent and penetrating. He placed his hand on Schulmeister's shoulder.

" You are an Alsatian? "

"Yes, sire."

"You look like a brave man — a man who will risk his life for France."

"Willingly," was the quick response.

After that the Man of Destiny and the former smuggler sat down and planned the scheme by which the Emperor was to gain the information he desired concerning the position, the extent and the prospective movements of the enemy. Schulmeister, while not particularly educated, was exceptionally quick witted. It has been said that he was as "sharp as a steel trap" and that is the impression he made on the Emperor, for Napoleon afterwards spoke glowingly of the spy to General Savery, his aide-de-camp.

The result of the campaign that had been planned was to have a marked effect upon the future of the "Little Corporal," as the idolizing soldiers insisted upon calling their chief. The Emperor accompanied the spy to the door of his headquarters, and as he left called after him:

"Don't fail me!"

Schulmeister hastened away and the thing that he remembered most of all was the figure of the little man in the long gray coat, waving his short arm and calling out that message of warning and of confidence. Who shall say that this day was not to mark the beginning of the founding of the great Napoleonic empire?

Time is everything!

Napoleon had said this often and his faithful servitor learned it by heart   He had a brief interview with General Savery, and the next moment started on his mission.   The expected happened — the thing he wished to happen — the incident that was necessary in order to set the little drama in motion.

He was arrested by the French police on the charge of espionage and hustled by them to the frontier.   It is impossible, if not indiscreet, to admit too many persons into one's confidence.   The officers who had made the arrest were ardent Frenchmen as well as faithful policemen, and they did not treat the young Alsatian any too tenderly.   In fact, he received more cuffs and kicks than he liked.   But he took them all unresistingly and even smiled when he was given a final push and sent headlong into the camp of the Austrians.

They received him with open arms, and when he told them a cock-and-bull story of his adventures in the French camp, nothing would do but that he must enter the Secret Service of the Austrian Army.   Such a valuable man was not to be lost.

The news of this was taken to the short man in the long gray coat, and as he paced up and down amidst his brilliantly uniformed officers he was heard to give vent to a chuckle — the sort of a chuckle one expects from a man whose plans are working precisely as he wished.

In the meantime Schulmeister settled down to business in earnest.   He gained the acquaintance and then the friendship of two very important men.   One was Captain Wend of the Austrian Secret Service, and the other Lieutenant Bendel, aide-de-camp to General Kienmayer.   In this, as in all else, he had followed the advice of his Corsican superior.   With him, as with the greater man, time was " everything."

A less audacious man would have hesitated about approaching such officers as Wend and Bendel; a less courageous man would have feared it, and a less imaginative man would never have thought of it. But Schulmeister had audacity, courage and imagination. He unbosomed himself to these two men, he pointed out the possibilities of the future and he painted the glories and the rewards of the Napoleonic empire.

In less than twenty-four hours Captain Wend and Lieutenant Bendel had become his allies, and thereafter worked with him hand and glove.

The next necessary move was to obtain the confidence of the higher Austrian officers and to find out their plans. He was able to do this with the assistance of Captain Wend and Lieutenant Bendel.

The Allies had a great body of soldiers in the field. The chief figure was Field Marshal Baron Mack, who had 90,000 splendidly equipped and well trained men under his command. His army formed the right wing of an enormous host, of which Archduke Charles with 140,000 men in northern Italy and Archduke John with 50,000 more in the passes of the Tyrol were important adjuncts.

General Mack was impressed with the great strength of his troops and felt that he could easily overcome Napoleon with the superiority of his numbers. Schulmeister learned of this over-confidence and was all the more anxious to reach the big man. Captain Wend undertook to present the Alsatian to Mack. It proved to be easy. The Austrian commander was not anx-

ious to move unless it was necessary, and when he
learned that there was a man in the vicinity who had
been in the camp of Napoleon he was eager to meet
him.

Schulmeister was bidden to come into his presence
and told to describe all that he had seen in the camp of
the "enemy." He did so with a vividness of imagination that would have done credit to Baron Mun-
chausen.

For nearly an hour the medium-sized man with the
ugly scars and the sky-blue eyes sat there and poured
fiction into the ears of the great general — the man
decorated with many medals and filled with a sense of
his own importance. And Mack believed it all. At
the conclusion the Austrian turned to one of his subordinates.

"You see; it is as I suspected. We must not move
from this place. We must watch and wait."

So, on the strength of the information — the false
information — supplied by the Alsatian smuggler, the
great army dawdled away its time in idleness. That
is to say, it was really idle while making a pretense of
activity. General Mack moved his troops about aim-
lessly in order to fool the enemy. That was his notion
of military strategy. But alas! for his expectations,
he was dealing with the master military strategist of
his time — if not of all times.

Having deluded the Austrian commander and
obtained accurate data concerning his plans, Schulmeister now made it his business to convey the information to Napoleon. He was readily given leave to go

to the French camp, with instructions to get all the facts possible as to its future movements.

He was in an enviable position. He had the passwords of both armies and he made his way to the quarters of the Emperor without any difficulty. As before, he found the silent, mysterious figure in the long gray coat, in the midst of his brilliantly attired staff. Schulmeister almost ran into the presence of the "Little Corporal."

"Sire," he said, "I have important news from the front."

Napoleon dismissed his officers, and sat down to listen to the report of the spy. His penetrating eyes seemed to pierce the soul of Schulmeister, but the Alsatian bore the scrutiny without flinching. The Emperor was satisfied His determined look gave way to one of his charming smiles.

"Proceed," said he.

Briefly, but without omitting any essential detail, Schulmeister told the story of his adventures from the time he had left the French camp until his return. At intervals there was a quiet chuckle from the great soldier. After he had concluded Napoleon propounded a number of questions, all of which the spy was able to answer clearly and satisfactorily. Then the short man in the long coat arose and paced up and down for some moments in silence. Presently he placed his hand on Schulmeister's shoulder and said:

"You have done your work well; return and keep me posted on future developments."

So Schulmeister made his way back to the Austrian

lines, while the Corsican proceeded with his plans for enveloping the enemy. Mack was "bottled up" but not quite effectively. Time was needed to complete the job and it was the Alsatian spy who was to make that time possible. He hastened to the Austrian commander. On this occasion he had no need of a go-between. He had now the confidence of Mack and the orders were that he should be permitted to go and come as he pleased. The Baron was delighted at the return of "his spy," as he called him. Schulmeister told of his visit to the French camp and gave what purported to be a résumé of Napoleon's plans.

The audacity of the man may be judged when it is known that he gave considerable accurate information. This was susceptible of confirmation, and the fact that it was confirmed by some of Mack's subordinates only served to raise Schulmeister in the estimation of the Austrian. And all the while Napoleon was marshaling his forces in such a way that the escape of the enemy seemed impossible.

Presently it began to dawn on General Mack that something was wrong. Disquieting reports came from the outer defenses. The Austrian became genuinely disturbed. He sent for Schulmeister and questioned him regarding the previous "information" he had brought him, but the Alsatian went through the ordeal with flying colors. Indeed, he gave him one or two additional facts which were so transparently correct that it placed the spy above suspicion.

On the seventh of October the campaign of strategy on both sides came to a close. With Napoleon it had been a series of restless moves. With Mack it had been a period of marking time, of doing nothing.

Too late he realized his mistake. He hurried to the north and found that the French troops were lihed up there in a solid phalanx; he turned to the south and discovered that his retreat was cut off there. The east and the west were in the same condition. The worst part of it was that these various lines were slowly but surely closing in on him. He could see now that the Corsican commander had been engaged in a vast enveloping campaign.

In a word, the great Napoleon had the Austrian army in a grip of steel!

Mack presented a pitiable sight, sitting there with his head between his hands, humiliated and remorseful — the victim of his own inactivity and his too confiding nature. The members of his staff gazed on the spectacle silently and not entirely with pity. From a distance Charles Louis Schulmeister also beheld the defeated Austrian chief. He felt, like the others, that it was all over but the shouting. The spy kept discreetly away from the immediate vicinity of the general and his staff. He knew very well that if his duplicity were discovered that he would, even then, be shot down like a dog. So he patiently awaited the arrival of the French troops.

But unexpectedly the situation seemed to change. It is an axiom of war that no chain is stronger than its weakest link. Napoleon had completely surrounded the Austrians and their allies, but there was one section where the French line was very thin — too thin indeed for French comfort.   And while Mack was moping over his hard fate some of his more energetic officers had been making a closer investigation of the situation.

The sound of a horse's hoofs was heard and an aide-de-camp galloped into the presence of Mack.

The officer alighted and saluted his chief.

" General," he cried, "there is a weak link in the French lines about two miles to the south, and with a sufficient force we may be able to break through."

This was as balm to the sorely afflicted pride of the Austrian.   He rose to the situation.   Officers were sent hither and thither and the soldiers massed for an attack upon the point in question.

Napoleon's spy looked upon these preparations with a sinking heart.   If they were carried out all of his work might go for naught.   What seemed like a glorious French victory might be turned into simply a drawn battle.

He had to think and think quickly!

As usual, he was equal to the occasion.   Captain Wend, of the Austrian Secret Service, and Lieutenant Bendel were near him ready to share in the downfall of the Austrian arms.   They, too, realized that the situation now hung upon a thread.   They were completely in Schulmeister's power, and were ready to do anything he might command.   He prepared a false message purporting to be signed by one of the officers of the outlying regiments.   It said, in substance:

'A revolution has broken out among the people of
Paris. Riots are going on in the streets. Napoleon
is hurrying home and the retreat of the French troops
is but a question of time.

This was conveyed to Mack by Captain Wend. It
filled the Austrian commander with amazement. It
was so unexpected and so surprising. His mind
worked slowly at best, and this intelligence seemed to
impair his thinking faculties still further. Schulmeister was too shrewd to permit his enterprise to rest
on a single warning. He sent a second message by
another officer and finally he personally appeared before the Austrian commander and told him things that
appeared like confirmation as strong as Holy Writ.
Mack was flooded with false messages.

As a consequence of this he called back his troops
and calmly sat down to await the retreat of the enemy.
That this inaction was largely due to his own indolence
cannot be doubted. But that it was chiefly prompted
by the cunning of the Alsatian spy is a matter of
history.

Before the sun went down that day the weak link in
the French lines had been strengthened effectively.
Napoleon had his troops under perfect control and the
ring of steel began to draw in closer and closer.
Mack, in his fancied security, waited for the retreat of
the enemy. Day by day Napoleon became more irre-
sistible, while the Austrian grew weaker.

Finally he awoke to discover that he had made a
second mistake, and a greater one than the first. The

Ulm campaign came to a sudden termination on the 18th of October, when Mack capitulated and surrendered his entire force.

This campaign has few parallels in history. Not a shot had been fired and many of the Austrians had not even seen a French soldier!

While the world was ringing with the news of this remarkable close to a remarkable campaign, General Savery, who is also known to history as the Duke de Rongo, accompanied Charles Louis Schulmeister on a visit to the Emperor Napoleon. The great soldier congratulated the Alsatian smuggler and loaded him down with financial favors. Schulmeister's fortune was made — from a worldly standpoint.

He was given leave of absence, with the understanding that he must remain subject to the Emperor's call. He had the right to go anywhere he chose and he chose to go to his home in the Alsatian village of New Freistell. The wife of his youth awaited him eagerly. This curious man, who knew neither fear nor pity, had one unexpected characteristic. He was passionately fond of children. Although married several years there was no prospect of little ones.

Schulmeister was not a man to be thwarted in his desires. He went out into the village, found two orphaned and homeless children and adopted them as his own. Visitors to the little place on the right bank of the Rhine tell of seeing the world-famous spy frolicking on the lawn of his home with these children. For the time being the man who had affected the des-

tinies of armies was subject to the whims and the
caprices of two little ones.   He obeyed their slightest
commands as implicitly as he had the orders of Napoleon Bonaparte.

Queer sight in this queerest of all possible worlds!

II

BELLE BOYD, THE CONFEDERATE GIRL WHO SAVED STONEWALL JACKSON

BELLE BOYD, THE CONFEDERATE GIRL
WHO SAVED STONEWALL JACKSON

THAT brilliant writer, Gilbert Chesterton, in one of his paradoxical essays said that a fact, if looked at fiercely, may become an adventure. It is certain that the most important facts in the life of Belle Boyd, the Confederate spy, constitute some of the most thrilling adventures in the great conflict between the sections — the Civil War in the United States.

She was only a girl when the flag was fired on at Sumter and her father and all the members of her family immediately enlisted in the Confederate army. When the Union troops took possession of Martinsburg, Belle Boyd found herself unwillingly inside the Federal lines. She had no formal commission from any of the Southern officers, but circumstances and her ardent nature made her an intense partisan of what was to be "The Lost Cause."

During the occupation of Martinsburg, she shot a Union soldier, who, she claimed, had insulted a Southern woman. From that moment until the close of the war she was actively engaged either as a spy, a scout or an emissary of the Confederacy. On more than one occasion she attracted the attention of Secretary of War Stanton, and although she served a term in a military prison, she seems to have been treated with unusual leniency. After the war she escaped to England, where she published her autobiography, bitterly assailing the victorious North.

It was in Martinsburg that Belle Boyd first began her work for the Confederacy. The Union officers sometimes left their swords and pistols about the houses which they occupied, and later were surprised and mystified at the strange disappearance of the weapons. They little thought that this mere slip of a girl was the culprit. Still later they were amazed to find that these same swords and pistols had found their way into the hands of the enemy and were being used against them.

But aside from this Belle Boyd made it her business to pick up all the information that was possible concerning the movements and the plans of the Union forces. Every scrap of news she obtained was promptly conveyed to General J. E. B. Stuart and other Confederate officers.

It was about the time of the battle of Bull Run that the Confederate general in command fixed upon Front Royal as a site for a military hospital. Belle Boyd was one of the nurses and many a fevered brow felt the touch of her cool hand and more than one stricken soldier afterwards testified to the loving care he received from this remarkable woman.

Later, Front Royal became the prize of the Union army, and Belle Boyd naturally fell under suspicion. Some remarks of her activities had already reached the

BELLE BOYD

front, and the officers kept her under close scrutiny. Fortunately, as she thought, she had been provided with a pass which would permit her to leave the place. Accordingly, the second day after the arrival of the Unionists she packed her grip and prepared to leave the town. As she came from the house she was halted by a Union officer named Captain Bannon.

" Is this Miss Belle Boyd? "

" Yes."

" Well, I am the Assistant Provost Marshal, and I regret to say that orders have been issued for your detention. It is my duty to inform you that you cannot proceed until your case has been investigated."

This did not suit the young woman at all. She opened her pocketbook and produced a bit of pasteboard.

" I have here a pass from General Shields. Surely that should be sufficient to permit me to leave the city."

The young officer was perplexed. He did not care to repudiate a pass issued by General Shields, and at the same time did not wish to disobey the instructions which he had received from his immediate chief.

" I hardly know what to do," he said. " However, I am going to Baltimore with a squad of men in the morning. I will take you with me and when we get there turn you over to General Dix."

This program was carried out and the Confederate spy was given a free trip to the monumental city, which she did not want. She was compelled to remain in Baltimore for some time, being kept constantly under the closest supervision. Finally, however, General Dix gave her permission to return to her home. There was no direct evidence against her and it was considered a waste of time and energy to keep her under guard. She was escorted to the boundaries of her old home by two Union soldiers. It was twilight when she arrived at the Shenandoah River. The effects of the war were to be seen on every side. The bridges had been destroyed, and they only managed to cross the river by means of a temporary ferry boat that had been pressed into service.

When she reached her home she found that it had been appropriated as a headquarters by General Shields and the members of his staff. He treated her courteously and said that no harm would befall her if she was discreet and attended to her own business. She was told that a small house adjoining the family dwelling had been set aside for her use, and that the soldiers would be given orders not to molest her in any way.

But the young daughter of the Confederacy kept her eyes and ears open and the night before the departure of General Shields, who was to give battle to General Jackson, she learned that a council of war was to be held in the drawing-room of the Boyd home. Just over this apartment was a bedroom containing a large closet. On the night of the council she managed to make her way to this room and slipped into the closet. A hole had been bored through the floor, whether by design or otherwise she was unable to tell. However, she immediately determined to take advantage of what she considered a providential situation.

When the council assembled the girl got down on her hands and knees in the bottom of the closet and placed her ear near the hole in the floor. To her great satisfaction she found that she could distinctly hear all of the conversation. The conference between the Union officers lasted for hours, but she remained motionless and silent until it had been concluded. When the scraping movement of the chairs on the floor below was heard she knew that everything was over so came out of her place of concealment. She was tired and her limbs were so stiff from remaining in that cramped position so long that it was all she could do to move. But she was full of grit and determination and as soon as the coast was clear she hurried across the courtyard and made the best of her way to her own room in the little house and wrote down in cipher — a cipher of her own — everything of importance that she had overheard.

After that it was but a matter of a few minutes to decide on her course of action. She knew that it would be extremely dangerous to call a servant or to do anything that might arouse the officers, who had by this time gone to bed, so she went to the stables and saddled a horse herself, and galloped away in the direction of the mountains. The moon was shining when she started on this wild ride. She had in her possession passes which she had obtained from time to time for Confederate soldiers who were returning south. Without them it would have been impossible for her to have

accomplished her purpose. Before she had gone a
half mile she was halted by a Federal sentry. He
grabbed the bridle of her horse and cried out:

" Where are you going? "

" I am going to visit a sick friend," was the ready
response.

" You can't do it," he cried.   " You ought to know
that you can't leave this place without a pass."

" But I have one," she said, with an engaging smile,
and drew out the piece of pasteboard.

The guard looked at it dubiously, but it was in
proper form and contained the necessary signature
and he grudgingly permitted her to continue on her
journey.

Twice again she was halted by sentinels and each
time she told the same story and underwent the same
experience. Once clear of the chain of sentries she
whipped her horse and hurried ahead for a distance of
fifteen miles. At that time the animal was in a perfect lather and when she pulled up in front of the
frame house which was the dwelling place of her
friends the horse was panting and trembling from the
unusual exertion. She leaped from the animal's back
and going to the door rapped on it with the butt end of
her riding whip. There was no reply, so she ham-
mered harder than ever. Presently a window in the
second story was cautiously opened and a head poked
out and a voice called:

" Who's there? "

" Belle Boyd, and I have important intelligence to
give to Colonel Ashby."

"My dear Belle!" shrieked the voice from the window. "Where in the world did you come from and how did you get here?"

"Oh, I forced the sentries," was the reply, in a matter of fact voice.

Within sixty seconds the girl was in the house and receiving refreshments and telling her strange story to her wondering friend. The horse in the meantime was taken to the stable by a negro and carefully groomed and fed. Only after these important details had been attended to was the girl permitted to tell her story.

"I must see Colonel Ashby," she said in conclusion, "and if you can tell me where to find him I will go at once."

She was informed that the Confederate officer and his party were in the woods about a half mile distant from the place in which they were sitting. Just as the girl was ready to go the front door was thrown open and Colonel Ashby stood before her. He looked at her as if she were a ghost and then finally burst forth in amazement:

"My God, Miss Belle, is that you? Where did you come from? Did you drop from the clouds?"

"No," she said smilingly, "I didn't. I came on horseback and I have some very important information."

Whereupon she related the details of the council that had taken place in the Boyd home, and then told the story of her mad ride through the night. She concluded by handing him the cipher, which he said would be communicated to his superior officers at once.

After that she insisted on mounting her horse and returning home again. It was more than two hours' ride, during which time she ran the blockade of the sleeping sentries with comparative success. Just at dawn when she was in sight of her home one of the sentries she was passing called out:

" Halt or I'll shoot ! "

But she did not halt. On the contrary she whipped her horse until it fairly leaped through the air. She felt that the man was leveling his gun in her direction. She lay flat on her horse's back with her arms around his neck, and this was done in the very nick of time, for at that same moment a hot bullet came singing past her ears. That was the only serious interruption. In a few minutes she had reached the grounds surrounding the Boyd home. Fortunately no one was in sight. She hurried into the house and went to bed in her aunt's room just at the break of dawn.

Two days later General Shields marched south with the idea of laying a trap to catch General Jackson. Once again the fearless girl determined to carry the information she possessed to her Confederate friends. Major Tyndale, at that time Provost Marshal, gave Belle Boyd and her cousin a pass to Winchester. Once there a gentleman of standing in the community called on her and handing her a package, said:

" Miss Belle, I am going to ask you to take these letters, and send them through the lines to the Confederate army. One of them is of supreme importance and I beseech you to try and get it safely to General Jackson."

After the exercise of considerable ingenuity she managed to get a pass to Front Royal. To add to the romantic feature of the business a young Union officer, who admired the girl, offered to escort her to her destination. They went in a carriage, but before starting she made it a point to conceal the Jackson letter inside her dress. The other letters, which were of comparatively small importance, she handed to the Union officer with the remark that she would take them from him when they reached Front Royal. On the way, as she feared, they were stopped by a sentinel. The Union admirer of the Confederate spy explained that they had a pass which would permit them to proceed on their way, but the zealous sentinel insisted on searching them and was highly indignant when he discovered the compromising letters in the hands cf the young man. He insisted upon confiscating them, but in the excitement forgot all about the girl, and she was permitted to go unmolested, carrying with her the precious letter intended for General Jackson.

Afterwards she laughingly expressed contrition for having involved an ardent admirer in such a serious plight, but excused herself on the ground that all was fair in war as well as in love. Fortunately, the young man, who was a perfectly loyal Northern soldier, was given the credit of having discovered the papers, which were valuable to his superior officers. Thus do we sometimes make a virtue of necessity.

After Belle Boyd had been in Front Royal for several days she learned that the Confederates were coming to that place, but she also discovered that General Banks was at Strasbourg with 4,000 men; that White was at Harper's Ferry; Shields and Geary a short distance away, and Frémont below the valley. At a spot which was the vital point all of the separate divisions were expected to meet and coöperate in the destruction of General Jackson. She realized that the Confederates were in a most critical situation and that unless the officers in command were aware of the facts they might rush into a trap which meant possible annihilation.

With characteristic promptness she decided on her plan of action. She rushed out to warn the approaching Confederates. On that occasion she wore a dark blue dress with a fancy white apron over it which made her a shining mark for bullets. The Federal pickets fired at her but missed and a shell burst near her at one time, but she threw herself flat on the ground and thus escaped what seemed to be sure death. Presently she came within sight of the approaching Confederates and waved her bonnet as a signal.

Major Harry Douglass, whom she knew, galloped up and received from her the information, which he immediately transmitted to General Jackson. The result of all this was a rout of the Union forces.

It was in this battle of Bull Run which followed soon afterwards that General Bee, as he rallied his men, shouted:

" There's Jackson standing like a stonewall! "

From that time, as has been aptly said, the name he received in a baptism of fire displaced that which he had received in a baptism of water.

The number of Union men engaged in the battle of Bull Run was about 18,000, and the number of Confederates somewhat greater.

Soon after the engagement the young woman received the following letter, which she prized until the hour of her death.

Miss Belle Boyd:

I thank you for myself and for the army, for the immense service you have rendered your country to-day.

Hastily, I am your friend,

T. J. Jackson, C. S. A.

Shortly before the close of the war Belle Boyd was captured and imprisoned. She escaped and made her way to England. In London she attracted the attention of George Augustus Sala, the famous writer. She had been married in the meantime and her husband, Lieutenant Hardage of the Confederate army, was among those taken prisoner by the Union forces.

While abroad she became financially embarrassed; indeed, at one time she was reduced to actual want. A stranger in a strange land, sick in mind and body, she was in a pitiable condition. Mr. Sala wrote a letter to the *London Times* explaining her sad state and roundly abusing the United States Government which had, he said, not only imprisoned her husband but was also "barbarous enough to place him in irons."

British sympathies were very strongly with the South at that time, and as a result of this plea provision was made for the immediate wants of the famous spy. After the war she disappeared from the public gaze, and some years later died in comparative obscurity.

III

THE INDIAN SCOUT WHO WAS THE
HERO OF KING PHILIP'S WAR

III

THE INDIAN SCOUT WHO WAS THE HERO OF KING PHILIP'S WAR

IT is a curious fact that Job Kattenanit, one of the Praying Indians of Deer Island, in Boston Harbor, should have emerged from King Philip's war with more glory than any other man, either white or red, who participated in that bloody contest.

Like the historic Biblical character from whom he received his name, Job was a sorely afflicted man. He was among the first group of Indians in that section of the United States to accept the Christian religion, and it was this fact, and in order to distinguish them from the other red men, that Kattenanit and his companions received the designation of the Praying Indians.

It is regrettable to record, however, that the excesses of some of the other natives had caused an indiscriminate hatred of the Indians throughout New England. They were regarded as wild beasts who should be shot and killed without mercy. It was while this feeling was at its height that Job Kattenanit and eleven of his companions were arrested on a charge of being concerned in the murder of seven white men. They were captured in the town of Lancaster and brought to Boston, tied "neck and neck," as the practice was in those primitive days.   The evidence against them was of the flimsiest character, and it was only through the efforts of Captain John Gookin, a magistrate who felt a special interest in the Indians, that their lives were spared and they were condemned to imprisonment on Deer Island.

In the meantime King Philip, the Indian chieftain, was spreading terror among the white people.   He was jealous of their gradual encroachment upon what he conceived to be his domain and he planned to destroy them.   He was a man of sagacity, although said to be wanting in physical courage, and he gradually combined all of the Indian tribes into one strong confederation and waited for a chance to strike the decisive blow.

It came at Swansea on Sunday, July 4, 1675.   The settlers were going to church when the Indians suddenly burst upon them.   But these pioneers were both pious and prepared, and taking up arms they routed their assailants.   Philip and his warriors then hunted the settlers in the Connecticut valley, burning down their homes and subjecting the people to the most atrocious forms of cruelty.   In the spring the war broke out anew along a frontier of three hundred miles and to within twenty miles of Boston.   The Indians had remained quiet for a long time after the initial outbreak — so quiet that the whites were thoroughly alarmed.   They knew the ruthless nature of their foes and they feared the consequences to the women and children if they should be taken unawares.

It was at this critical stage of affairs that Major
Gookin — he had been promoted — bethought himself
of the Praying Indians on Deer Island.   It was absolutely necessary to know something of the plans of
King Philip and·his bloodthirsty redskins.   If a white
man went into their camp he was certain to be scalped
and tortured.   If an Indian could be induced to act as
a spy he might save the whites from a wholesale massacre.

The eloquent Major visited Deer Island and presented these facts to the prisoners and called for volunteers.   He said that a service of this kind would
not only secure the release of the Praying Indians, but
would win for them the lasting friendship of the white
people.

" I go," said one handsome brave, rising and lifting
his hand solemnly in mid-air.   " I go, not for reward,
but to save the palefaces from death."

The Indian was Job Kattenanit.   He was tall and
perfectly erect, with piercing black eyes and a grave,
almost sorrowful countenance.   There was a suggestion of nobility in his bearing.   In short, he might
well have·passed for the original of Deerfoot, so viv-
idly pictured by James Fenimore Cooper.

Major Gookin recognized him at once.   He knew
the Indians personally, and he had a special friendship
for this straight shouldered chap.   He rushed over and
gripped him by the hand.

" Job," he exclaimed, " the white people shall know
of this and in time it will help your people."

A mist passed before the bright eyes of the Indian,

and he gave a gesture as if to sweep the suggestion aside.

" White man cruel to Indian," he rejoined, " but the red man must return good for evil."

As they were about to leave another Indian rose in his place and said:

" Me go, too — me go with Job."

This was James Quannapohit, a native in whom Major Gookin also had implicit confidence. After deliberation he decided to accept the services of both volunteers. They were taken aside and given careful directions.

That night Job and James were brought secretly from Deer Island and set free — according to arrangement. In order to avoid difficulties they had been first escorted beyond the British lines.

From that point they journeyed alone and on foot. It was a long walk, and when they reached their destination they were footsore, hungry and almost in rags. It was as they wished.   They bore the appearance of fugitives, of escaped prisoners. It was daybreak when they arrived in the camp of the Nipmuck Indians. They threw themselves on their faces and begged for food and drink. The amazed redskins who surrounded them wanted to know who they were and what they were doing in the camp of the Nipmuck Indians. Job, who acted as spokesman, insisted upon refreshments and said he would tell his story to some one in authority. After their wants had been satisfied they were escorted to Mantampe, a chief Sachem of the tribe.

"What you do here?" he demanded.

"We have escaped from the clutches of the white man," replied Job in his native tongue, "and we came to you for protection. The white man of Lancaster came and took the red man prisoner. He charged us with murdering his squaws and he gave us no chance to defend ourselves."

"Tell me more," said the chief Sachem, deeply interested.

Job did as he was requested and he was able to do so all the more eloquently because he was giving an account of some things that had actually occurred to the Praying Indians. He said they had been accused by David, a fellow savage, of being concerned in the murder of the whites. But he added that the manner in which David was forced to make this charge robbed it of all value. He related how Colonel Mosely and a scouting party captured David and tied him to a tree; how with six muskets pointed at his head he was told to confess or die. To save his life he named eleven men he understood were present at the murder, though he himself was not there, and knew nothing about it. The men were put on trial, and so great and indiscriminate was the popular feeling against the natives that several of them were condemned.

"But you are alive," grinned the Sachem.

Job admitted the soft impeachment and explained how he and his companions had been imprisoned on Deer Island. He said that he and James Quannapohit had managed to escape, but slyly enough neglected to tell the Sachem that the escape had been arranged by

their English friends. He concluded by saying that
they had come to the camp of the Nipmuck Indians to
get the lay of the land, " so that they might advise the
friends they had left if it would be possible for them
also to escape."

The Sachem accepted the story of Job and his companion and they were given the liberty of the camp.
The two Praying Indians kept their eyes and ears open
and learned much. Mantampe was undoubtedly in
command of a large force. Job met many of the
Indians, who were, as a rule, able fighting men,
straight as arrows, very tall and active.

Three squaws who were in the camp interested and
amused the spies. One was a very proud dame. She
spent the best part of each day in dressing herself in
all the colors of the rainbow; she powdered her hair
and painted her face, wore numberless necklaces, had
jewels in her hair and bracelets on her wrists. When
she finished her toilet she sat down and spent the
remainder of the day in making girdles of wampum
and beads.

James Quannapohit found great favor in the eyes
of Mantampe. He made him share his tent with
him and insisted upon his repeating the story of his
escape from Deer Island. During the course of these
talks James learned that the Nipmuck Indians contemplated a raid on the white settlers. They proposed to
burn Lancaster and then attack other towns. The
method of the raid was not made clear. One morning
Mantampe called James before him.

" Son," he said in substance, " I am about to take a

journey for the purpose of visiting the big chief, King Philip. If all goes well I may take you with me."

This alarmed James. He dreaded the idea of going further into the Indian country, perhaps to a point where it would be impossible for him to make his escape. Besides that he had a good reason for wishing to avoid a meeting with the king. He had once fought against Philip at Mount Hope. He had taken a conspicuous part in the battle and he knew that if the King recognized him he would be shot.

The next morning he arose before any one was stirring, and left the camp. He urged Job to go along with him but the other spy refused to do so.

"But you will be killed," urged James, "when they discover my absence. They will at once suspect that you are a spy, and that means death."

Job shook his head.

"You go," he said. "I don't blame you for that. But I am going to stay for a while. It may mean life or death, but I am willing to take my chances."

Nothing that James could say would shake the determination of Job. So the younger Indian started on the return journey to Boston alone. There had been severe storms and the snow lay deep on the ground. It was necessary for the Indian to wear heavy snowshoes and this made traveling all the more difficult.

When the Indian spy reached Boston he had a tale of unparalleled hardships to relate to his white friends. But more important than that was his story of the plans of the Indians against the settlers in and around Lan-

caster.   He was highly praised for the effective work
he had done and was showered with attentions by the
white men and their families.   For the first time since
the beginning of what is popularly known as King
Philip's war an Indian was treated as though he were
a human being.

Indeed, it is no exaggeration to state that the exploit
of the two Indians did more to reinstate the redskins
in the good graces of the whites than anything that
had occurred in years.

But curiously enough the settlers did little or nothing
to protect themselves against the expected attack.   The
very warning which should have put them on their
guard seemed to lull them into a false sense of security.
There were two reasons for this.   The first one was
that the suspected danger was comparatively remote
— a matter of weeks in fact.   Another and more important one was the desire to get further and fuller
information from the other Indian scout.   Job was the
shrewder and more capable of the two messengers.   It
was just possible that the abrupt departure of James
might arouse the suspicion of the savages and cause
them to entirely revise their plans.   James was closely
questioned concerning his companion.

"Why didn't he come back with you?" he was
asked.

James shrugged his shoulders and threw out his
hands in a gesture of hopelessness.

"He very stubborn man.   Have his own way.
No listen to poor James."

"Do you think he intends to come back?"

At this suggestion of possible disloyalty on the part
of his friend the Indian became very indignant.   He
was so angry that he found it impossible to express
himself coherently.   But his manner, if not his words,
perfectly satisfied the questioner of the perfect good
faith of Job.   As a matter of fact it was never
seriously doubted and the white man who propounded
the query felt ashamed at having put the unworthy
suspicion into words.

In the meantime Job found himself in an embarrass-
ing and really dangerous situation.   With the flight
of James the savages, for the first time, became skeptical concerning the motives of the two visitors.   The
chief Sachem sent for Job and put him through a
severe cross-examination.   But Job was shrewd and
told them a cock-and-bull story that satisfied their
curiosity.   As a result of this he was treated with even
more consideration than when he first arrived in camp.
He was fearful lest the Sachem should want him to
accompany him on the proposed visit to King Philip.
He knew that to go before the big Chief would be
taking his life in his hands.   Finally, to his great joy,
the Sachem decided that he should not go on the trip.

The next three days were days of great anxiety to
the spy.   He knew that the emissary to the King would
bring final plans for the attack on the whites and he
was fearful lest anything should happen to deprive
him of this much needed information.   So he exerted
himself to the utmost in order to keep the good will of
the savages.   As a result of this they virtually took
him to their bosoms.   In speaking of this afterwards

he said that he felt no compunctions of conscience. He did not feel that he was betraying them but rather that he was engaged in an honest attempt to save human life.

He took part in their amusements, which helped to while away the time. One of the most popular of the games was called " hunt the button," a diversion somewhat akin to that which is enjoyed by children the world over. This was played at night when the natives, in paint and buckskin, seated themselves around a tepee, with the fire blazing bright in their faces, as they swung their hands in time with a rhythmic chant. This was indulged in by both sexes. Also they played the game of " deer-foot." In this a number of cylindrical bones, usually taken from the foot of the deer, and perforated with several holes around their sides, were strung on a cord, which had at one end several strands of beads and at the other a long needle. The object was to toss the string, with the beads upon it, in such a way as to catch in the point of the needle, which was retained in the hand, any designated one of the bones or bead strands.

But presently the Sachem returned from his visit to the King and from the air of activity which prevailed Job realized that something important was on hand. It did not take him long to find out that that something was war. Clubs that were armed with jagged teeth of stone were brought from their hiding places and sharpened. Javelins, lances and arrows became very much in evidence. The arrows were most numerous. They were made of hard wood and with a feather from the

KING PHILIP, OR METACOMET.

eagle. These various weapons were not unknown to
Job, of course, but his own tribe was composed of
more peace-loving Indians and they were not in the
habit of using the more destructive weapons.

Finally one night the Sachem gathered the most important men of the tribe about him and outlined the
plans of King Philip. Job, who was still in the confidence of the savages, was permitted to hear all that
was said. The proposal was shocking, even to a redskin. The intention was to destroy the whites at one
blow, if that were possible. The day and the hour at
which the descent was to be made upon Lancaster was
fixed and the method of attack outlined. This was
news indeed, and vastly more important than that
which had been carried to Boston by James.

Job Kattenanit knew that the hour had come to act.
With haste he would have time to warn the threatened
settlers, but with not a minute to spare. Creeping
away, he made for the edge of the camp. Fortunately
most of the Indians — aside from those who were at-
tending the council of war — were asleep. He passed
one sentinel unobserved and gained the fringe of the
encampment in safety. The road to Boston was familiar to him and he counted on reaching there by dusk
on the evening of February 8th.

But just as he struck the main road leading to his
destination there was a cry of anger and dismay from
the Nipmuck camp.

His flight had been discovered.

Instead of halting he redoubled his speed. From
time to time he heard savage cries and he knew that

he was being pursued. The thought of giving up never once entered his mind. It was too late to retreat now. The Nipmuck Indians had been credulous enough, but it would be impossible to deceive them any longer. Job was in fine physical condition and he ran with the swiftness of a deer. But his enemies were equally fleet-footed and it seemed only a question of time when he would be overtaken. Nearer and nearer came the footsteps in the rear. He felt that there must be a number of Indians in the party, but evidently they did not have time to give a general alarm.

Just when he was congratulating himself on the possibility of outrunning his pursuers an arrow whizzed past his head. This was a new danger and one that he had not anticipated. He paused for a second and turned to look at the men who were after him. Instantly a well-directed arrow struck him in the chest within an inch of the region of the heart.

A heavy blanket covered the fleeing redskin, and with that momentary pause and turn the arrow had penetrated the covering. But, as by a miracle, it went no further. The Praying Indian wore a metal charm on his breast, suspended by a string fastened about his neck. That saved his life.

In that trying moment the shrewd Indian made his resolution. To pull the arrow out and run ahead again only meant postponing the inevitable. Instead of that, he paused motionless for a second, then swayed to and fro, and fell flat on his back.

Everything depended upon the success of this ruse. It was, perhaps, half a minute before the Nipmuck

Indians came up, and when they did they regarded the motionless body with something like awe. Job suppressed his breathing as much as possible. Two of the pursuers engaged in an animated conversation, and finally turning, retraced their steps, leaving the spy for dead.

He lay there perfectly quiet until he was sure they were out of sight. Then he jumped up and resumed his interrupted flight. The story of that journey through a wilderness in the most inclement season of the year should rank with the classics of adventure. But only the savage himself knew what he was compelled to undergo, and he never spoke of it afterwards.

He arrived at Major Gookin's house late on the night of February 9th. His feet were bruised and bleeding from the long trip and he was faint from weakness on account of exposure and want of food. All of the inmates at the Gookin dwelling were asleep and Job had to rap repeatedly on the door to awaken them. Presently the Major came downstairs and the meeting between the two — white man and the red — was most affecting.

The tidings he brought were startling. It was evident that it would only be a question of hours before the settlers were attacked. Major Gookin did not return to his bed that night. He dispatched messengers to all of the surrounding towns. In an incredibly short time troops were marching from everywhere to the aid of the threatened town. Captain Wadsworth, at Marlborough, received the news at daybreak and started for Lancaster at once. Others did the same thing.

The savages came over four hundred strong. Re-enforcements added to this number. The white men were not so numerous, but they fought with a courage born of desperation. The town was partially destroyed by fire and a few of the people taken prisoners by the Indians. Had it not been for the warning of Job Kattenanit there would have been a wholesale massacre and Lancaster would have been left in ashes.

That was the beginning of the end. Driven to drastic measures by the atrocities of the savages, the settlers hunted down the Indians like wild beasts. King Philip was driven from one hiding place to another, going finally to his old home on Mount Hope, Rhode Island, where he was shot by a faithless Indian, August 12, 1676.

But Job Kattenanit, the Praying Indian, did more than any white man to break up the reign of terror caused by the savages, and even though history fails to mention the fact, he was the real hero of King Philip's War.

IV

HOW THE SUICIDE OF A STAFF OFFICER ONCE AVERTED WAR BETWEEN AUSTRIA AND RUSSIA

IV

HOW THE SUICIDE OF A STAFF OFFICER ONCE AVERTED WAR BETWEEN AUSTRIA AND RUSSIA

COULD the preservation of the life of an officer of the Austrian army on May 26, 1913, have prevented the devastating war in Europe that followed? And if the same man had lived would it have precipitated a war at that time between Austria and Russia?

These questions may remain unanswered to the end of time, but there are students of history who do not hesitate to give an affirmative reply to each of the momentous queries.

The story of Colonel Albert Riddle — that is near enough to his real name to make it clear to those who were within the inner circle and far enough away to protect the feelings of his descendants who are still living — is one of the strangest in history. In its way it takes its place with the Mystery of the Man in the Iron Mask, although in the present case there was never any question of the identity of the victim or of the fact of his death.

Colonel Riddle was connected with the general staff of the Eighth Army Corps. He was one of the favorites of the Austrian Court. He was young,

handsome, attractive and with a dash and go about
him that made him a general favorite. He had won
an enviable record for bravery in battle, and was considered an efficient officer in every sense of the term.

Presently the time came when it was desirable to
learn something concerning the secrets of the Russian
army plans.   Austria, like all other great countries in
Europe, had any number of spies, but very few of
them were available for the character of work which
would be necessary in order to learn the plans of the
higher military officers of the Russian Empire.   It
was in this emergency that Colonel Riddle was called
upon.   He had a young soldier's love of adventure
and he eagerly volunteered for the delicate and difficult
task.   He was well supplied with money and authority
and eventually he went to St. Petersburg, where he
posed as a sort of military attaché of the Austrian
embassy.   The social side of life in St. Petersburg
attracted him immensely and while he devoted part of
his time to the work for which he had been assigned,
he nevertheless found numerous opportunities for sat-
isfying his love for the pleasant things of life.

Indeed, so genial did he find his surroundings, that
he had little or no desire to return home.   He became
very popular with the ladies of the Russian Court, and
participated in many of the social events for which
that capital was noted.

But everything has its end, and finally the day came
when it was deemed necessary for him to return to
Vienna.   He reached Austria in due time and made a
comprehensive report of his discoveries, a report that

was considered acceptable by the higher officers of the Austrian army. After that he retired to his home in Prague, Bohemia. He had many friends there and indulged in what was regarded as a well earned rest. His activities — his military activities — were suspended for the time being, and this high grade spy enjoyed life with more zest than is granted to the ordinary or commonplace person.

But suddenly and as unexpectedly as a bolt from the blue sky came the report that Colonel Riddle was suspected of treason to his country.

He was summoned to Vienna to defend himself from the charges. Now whether they were true or not never has been and never will be definitely determined. At all events the military and social circles of the gayest capital in the world were filled with stories which were not creditable to the fascinating and really popular colonel. These stories, it may be stated with surety, lost nothing in the telling, and as they went from mouth to mouth they assumed proportions which represented Riddle as being one of the most marvelous deceivers of his time.

In the meanwhile the talk took on a new twist. It was contended that if Colonel Riddle lived to be prosecuted for treason the revelations at his trial would make it impossible for Austria to maintain friendly relations with Russia. The gossip said more than that; it said that not only relations with Russia would be broken, but that the bonds between Austria and one of her fully trusted allies would be severely strained. As a matter of fact, there is no telling to what extent

Germany and Austria might have found reason to suspect each other had Colonel Riddle gone on the stand
and made the revelations which would have been
necessary in order for him to defend himself on the
charge of treason.   He was accused by unknown accusers of not only giving military secrets of Austria
and Germany to Russia, but also of having betrayed
to Russia the Russian officers who were selling Russia's military secrets to Austria and Germany.   Those
who were acquainted with the man were vehement in
denying his guilt of any such double faced dealings.
At all events, one of the secrets of this talk was that
Austria and Germany very materially revised their
plans for mobilizing their forces along the Russian
frontier.

In the meantime, while Colonel Riddle was in Vienna preparing for the court-martial, the Government
had its agents in Bohemia collecting evidence to be
used against the accused man.   Two of the secret
service men who were in Prague burst into his room
for the purpose of securing any information that
might be obtained there.   At first it looked as if they
were to have their labors for their pains.   Nothing
out of the ordinary was found.   It was a sort of
apartment that might be expected to belong to a comparatively wealthy and popular young man.   There
were trophies from all parts of the world; souvenirs
of his stay at St. Petersburg — this, it must be remembered, was before the days that the capital of Russia
assumed the unfamiliar name of Petrograd — and
other interesting places.   There were numerous pri-

vate letters, some of them tender love missives. But
at the last moment the secret service men discovered
a private desk in a corner of the room which, when
broken open, disclosed a number of papers of an incriminating character. It was positively declared at
the time that if certain of these papers ever became
public nothing could prevent a war between Austria
and Russia.

And here another curious twist is introduced in this
strangest of strange stories. It was asserted in a way
that gave it the appearance of verity that some of the
papers, had they come to light, would have ruptured,
if not entirely broken, the relations between Austria
and Germany. Even at that time these two countries
were looked upon as the Siamese twins among the nations of Europe. The Austrian authorities were seriously alarmed. They could not contemplate a struggle
between their own country and their German ally with
equanimity. The question was what to do under these
critical circumstances. One of the first things was to
take charge of all of the possessions of the unfortunate
man. Everything was seized — not only the official
papers, but private letters, tailors' bills, photographs,
and all other articles that were found in the room.
Not only were the papers seized and sequestered, but
his apartments were sealed, thus concluding the first
act in the tragic drama.

But the most serious part of the business was still
to come. The papers were out of the way; there was
no documentary evidence in the case, but the man still
remained, and what he might do or say was the un-

known quantity in the problem. The strangest part of
the queer affair was that in spite of all of these charges
and counter charges against the fascinating colonel he
was still looked upon as a most patriotic person. It
was assumed — and probably with correctness — that
while he had been indiscreet and possibly blameworthy,
he never really intended to betray his own country.
Anyhow the cold facts remained. It was a condition
and not a theory which confronted those in authority.
The court-martial had been ordered. It was fixed for
a certain day. If it took place according to schedule
it might strike the spark which would cause a terrific
explosion in Europe. If it were postponed, how could
the postponement be explained? And even if it were,
there would still remain the man who had been indiscreet and who might be again.

It was at this stage of events that Colonel Riddle,
who was kept in strict confinement, received a call from
two of his fellow officers. They smoked and chatted,
and even had a glass of wine together. All of the
facts were placed before him in an orderly manner.
He was shown that he could not escape under any
circumstances and that if he should live, the life of the
empire might be threatened. It was the existence of
one or the other. He was told, as he knew very well,
that any attempt to defend himself would place Austria
in the position of having attempted to steal the military
secrets of Russia, and further, of being faithless to
Germany. Finally, about midnight, they parted, and
as the officers left the room one of them with a significant gesture handed Colonel Riddle a loaded pistol.

The next morning when the guard made his regular rounds his eyes met a shocking sight. Colonel Riddle lay prostrate on the floor with a bullet wound in his forehead. The pistol with which the deed was committed lay by his side.

There was much regret, of course. The highest officials of the Austrian Court were heard to express sorrow at the untimely taking off of the popular young officer. His high standing, his unusual ability and his bright prospects for the future only made the tragedy the sadder.

A five line cablegram told the story to America. It is doubtful if one person in a thousand either read it or paid any attention to it. It was simply reported as the suicide of a soldier who was about to be placed on trial for treason. What could be more natural than that a man in the face of impending disgrace — especially when he had been a trusted officer — should take his life? Such things had happened before. Why should it excite any comment?

In the early part of the following month there were whispers concerning the real facts that lay behind the curious story of Colonel Riddle's suicide. These facts came to light little by little, and finally were woven into a coherent and connected story. Many friends of the dead soldier, who knew that he had fought bravely for his country and had acted as a spy in her interests, also knew that he had become a martyr for the Fatherland.

One of the results of the tragic affair was a reorganization of the entire spy system of the Austrian army.

Secrets which had hitherto been known to a score of men were now confined to a comparative few.   Every man was placed under suspicion, and even spies whose fidelity had never been questioned before were subjected to the closest scrutiny of other spies whose existence was unknown to them.   At the same time the German secret service was reorganized and put in position where the likelihood of a betrayal of state secrets was exceedingly improbable.   Even those who were unwilling to believe that Colonel Riddle had been guilty of treason admitted that the looseness of the spy system placed it within the power of many men to betray those for whom they were supposed to be working.

"The Government," said one officer, alluding to the tragedy that had just occurred, "found it imperatively necessary to close the mouth of one of its own sons.   I hope the necessity for such a thing will never occur again."

Germany has never expressed itself officially in this matter, but those who know a thing or two about military methods may be sure that the important officers in that country fully approved of the manner in which this unfortunate incident was handled.   Experience has proved that there is no way to keep military secrets, that there is no protection against the weakness or cupidity of your own spies.   Only one man can be trusted with a mobilization plan, and that man is the chief of the general staff.   If he fails it is madness to put him on trial.   The only reasonable thing to do under the circumstances is to have him efface himself from the earth. Exile is impossible. Death is the only remedy.

Such were the arguments that were used a little over two years ago in order to justify the Riddle case. Since that time dispatches have been coming from Germany, Austria, Italy and various other countries reporting vaguely that documents have been sequestered at the postoffices in these places and that those responsible for their existence have been subjected to drastic military discipline. That, it may be safe to say, means that those who know too much have had to answer with their lives for their indiscretion.

In a short while after the death of Colonel Riddle the incident was forgotten, and so far as people are concerned was relegated to the lumber room of unsolved mysteries — and to that hazy and uncertain section of history which is filled with stories that everybody believes and no one is willing to affirm. But it seems curious indeed that two years after a life had been sacrificed in order to avert war, the nations of Europe should be engaged in a death grapple.

War, like politics, makes strange bedfellows. The fate of nations often rests on the tossing of a coin. Human lives are but the pawns with which the kings and emperors play the game. This was pathetically illustrated in the case of Colonel Albert Riddle. By snuffing out his own life he prevented war between two great empires. And yet, as if by the decree of Nemesis, the Goddess of Justice, these same countries were soon clutching at the throat of one another.

V

THE ROMANTIC SIDE OF MAJOR ANDRÉ'S UNSUCCESSFUL EXPLOIT

V

THE ROMANTIC SIDE OF MAJOR ANDRÉ'S
UNSUCCESSFUL EXPLOIT

ALL the world loves a lover, and the fact that the
unfortunate Major John André was engaged to
be married to a charming English girl at the
time of his execution helped to place him in something
like a romantic light before the world. He had
another advantage. The blackness of the treason of
Benedict Arnold made André shine by comparison, so
that while the American was regarded with horror and
contempt everywhere, the unhappy fate of the young
Englishman excited universal sympathy.

It was in 1769 that André met Miss Honora Sneyd
in Litchfield, England. It was a case of love at first
sight, ardent and impetuous on both sides. But, alas, as
is usual, the course of true love did not run smoothly.
The match was disapproved by Miss Sneyd's father,
and the young man was told to keep away from the
house of his adored one. To make assurance doubly
sure he was sent to his father's counting house in London. He tried hard to accustom himself to office
drudgery, but in spite of his best intentions the face of
Honora kept popping up from amidst the rows of
figures, and upsetting his calculations.

His was an adventurous spirit, and in 1771 he tossed aside his ledgers and day books to accept a commission in a regiment bound for America. There was an affecting scene when he parted from Miss Sneyd and she gave him her portrait as a souvenir. He plighted his troth anew and promised that the picture should never part from him under any circumstances — a promise that was kept with pathetic fidelity.

Before he had been in America long André, by reason of his courage and intelligence, rose to the position of aide-de-camp to Sir Henry Clinton, commander-in-chief of the British forces. It was at this juncture that Benedict Arnold, smarting under supposed wrongs, made a proposition to the British to betray to them the post at West Point, of which he was in command. It was regarded as the key to the American position and General Clinton designated Major André as the man to conduct the negotiations with the traitor Arnold. The importance of this position was equaled by its danger.

The conspiracy between Arnold and André had been carried on by means of correspondence for quite a while. They wrote under fictitious names, and naturally the greatest secrecy was observed. But finally the time came when it was necessary to hold a personal meeting in order to bring the treason to a head. Major André at that time held the position of adjutant general in the British army, and it was at Arnold's request that he was detailed to meet the traitorous general for the purpose of settling all the details. On the 20th of September, 1780, André went on board the

British sloop of war *Vulture* with Colonel Beverly Robinson, and proceeded up the Hudson with a view of holding an interview with Arnold. There is a strong feeling, or at least circumstantial evidence, which indicates that Robinson was partially responsible for bringing Arnold to the state of mind where he was willing to sacrifice his country in order to satisfy his own wounded vanity. At all events, they made the trip together and on the night of the 21st a boat was sent by Arnold to the *Vulture* which brought André to the shore about six miles below Stony Point.

In a secluded spot and after midnight the conspirators met and prepared the plans by which the American cause was to be betrayed. Daylight appeared and still the conference went on. It was suggested that it would be desirable to have breakfast, and at Arnold's invitation André consented to accompany him to the house of Joshua Smith, which was about two miles below the meeting place. They sat there for a long time and presently the booming of cannon was heard and they saw that the *Vulture* had weighed anchor and was proceeding down the river. This was due to the fact that Colonel Livingston of the American army thought that she was too near the American outposts, and with characteristic promptness he brought cannon to bear on the vessel and compelled her to descend the river.

This interfered seriously with the scheme that had been agreed upon between the Englishman and the American. Plans of the American works, their armament, the number of troops they contained and other important details were handed by Arnold to André. To make sure that he should not lose the precious papers Major André took off his boots and placed the documents between his stockings and his feet. As it was evident that André would not be able to reach the *Vulture* Arnold furnished him with a horse and gave him a pass which directed the guards to permit him to go where he pleased on the ground that he was engaged in public business. A similar pass was given to Joshua Smith who had acted as host to the spy and the traitor. Major André passed the entire day at Smith's house in the hope and expectation of being able to get aboard the *Vulture* at night, but when evening arrived Smith became frightened and declined to row out to the *Vulture*. He proposed instead to cross the river with André and then see that he was put on the road by which he might return to New York. The Englishman was greatly disappointed, but was finally induced to throw Smith's overcoat over his uniform, and shortly before dusk they started to go across at Kings Ferry. They succeeded in making about eight miles on the other side when they were stopped by an American sentinel. Arnold's pass satisfied the officer in command but he warned them against proceeding any farther at night.

They remained at a farmhouse until morning and by that time had now approached a portion of the country some thirty miles in extent which lay between the lines of the opposing armies and was considered neutral ground. After proceding three miles farther toward New York André and his host breakfasted at a farm-

THE MEETING BETWEEN BENEDICT ARNOLD AND MAJOR ANDRÉ

house and then parted. Smith returned home and
André continued on his way to New York, confident
that he was past all danger and that it was only a question of time when the treason of Arnold would be
completed.

He was going through a wooded glen when he was
suddenly confronted by three men, the first of whom,
was clothed in a manner which might suggest his connection with the British army.

" Good morning," exclaimed André, imprudently.
" Gentlemen, I hope you belong to our party."

" What party? " asked the leader of the trio.

" The lower party," said André, indicating the camp
of the British army.

" We do," said the leader, but with a significant look
at his companions.

The young Englishman was now entirely off his
guard and declared himself to be a British officer.   He
said that he had been up the country on most important
business and must not be detained on any account.   He
drew out his gold watch as evidence of his statement,
but to his surprise, the foremost of the young men
clutched him by the shoulder and exclaimed:

" You are our prisoner! "

It afterwards became known that the three men
were farmers of the neighborhood, their names being
John Paulding, Isaac Van Wort and David Williams.
Paulding happened by chance to be wearing an overcoat
that had been left on his place by a British soldier, and
it was this uniform that had misled André.

The English major was very much exercised by this

time and now remembered his pass. He exhibited the paper that had been given to him by General Arnold, saying:

" You see that I am all right. This pass permits me to go through the lines."

Paulding, however, was convinced that there was something wrong. He seized the bridle of André's horse and compelled him to dismount and then subjected him to a very close search. They took off his boots and his stockings and found the concealed papers. Paulding read them carefully and as he came across the incriminating words exclaimed:

" My God, he is a spy!"

The Englishman used all of his persuasive powers on his captors, but in vain. He offered them any amount of money if they would release him, but they refused and conducted their prisoner to Lieutenant Colonel Jameson, who was in command of the post at New Castle. He in turn instantly sent the papers found in André's possession by express to General Washington, who was then returning from a visit to the French at Hartford.

By a curious chain of circumstances Washington was returning with the members of his own military family, including General Lafayette and General Knox. On the morning of the 25th of September he sent a messenger to General Arnold saying that the party would breakfast with him on that day. As they approached Arnold's headquarters at the Robinson house Washington turned aside from the direct route in order to visit the defenses on the east side of the Hudson.

Lafayette, with the proverbial politeness of the French, suggested that Mrs. Arnold would be waiting breakfast for them.

" Ah," replied Washington, " you young men are all in love with Mrs. Arnold.   I see that you are eager to be with her as soon as possible.   Go and breakfast with her and tell her not to wait for me!   I must ride down and examine the redoubts on this side of the river.   I will be with you shortly."

His request was complied with.   Lafayette and his friends found Mrs. Arnold — who was the famous Peggy Shippen — as usual, bright, gay and fascinating.   Arnold himself was strangely grave and thoughtful.   In the very midst of the breakfast a horseman galloped to the door and gave a letter to Arnold, which stated that André was a prisoner and that the papers found in his boots had been forwarded to General Washington.   Arnold was compelled to act quickly in this crisis and he gave remarkable evidence of quickness of mind.

" Gentlemen," he said to his guests, " I am compelled to leave you for a time and hope that I may be excused."

From the breakfast room he hurried to Mrs. Arnold's apartments, and when she came to him in response to his summons explained his position, saying: " I must fly instantly.   My life depends on my reaching the British lines without detection."

It was perhaps a few hours after this that the letters and papers which told the story of Arnold's perfidy were handed to Washington.   Washington read them

calmly and, calling Lafayette and Knox, told them the
story, adding sadly:

" Who can we trust now? "

Hot on the heels of this came one from Major André
explaining his position and saying that he had been
betrayed into the vile condition of an enemy in disguise within the American posts. He asked that in
any rigor policy might dictate he should not be branded
with anything dishonorable, as he considered himself a
messenger in the service of the king and not an involuntary impostor. He said that he wrote to vindicate
his fame and not to solicit security. To this letter
Washington made no reply.

On the 26th of September Major Tallmadge, having
André in custody, arrived at the Robinson house.
General Washington declined to see the prisoner but
gave orders that he should be treated with every courtesy and civility consistent with his absolute security.

The charming personality of the prisoner won for
him the personal regard of all with whom he was
brought into contact. His immediate jailor said that
it often drew tears from his eyes to find André so
agreeable in conversation on different subjects while
he — the American officer — was reflecting on the
future fate of the young Englishman.

While Tallmadge was on the way with André to the
American headquarters their conversation became very
frank and their relations friendly. Presently André
asked Tallmadge with what light he would be regarded
by General Washington at a military tribunal. The

American hesitated, but when André repeated the question he said:

"I had a much loved chum in Yale College by the name of Nathan Hale, who entered the army in 1775. Immediately before the battle of Long Island General Washington wanted information respecting the strength, position and probable movements of the enemy. Captain Hale volunteered his services, went over to Brooklyn and was taken just as he was passing the outposts of the enemy on his return. Do you remember the sequel of the story?"

"Yes," said André, in a low voice that was tremulous with emotion. "He was hanged as a spy. But you surely do not consider his case and mine alike."

"Yes, precisely similar," said Major Tallmadge, "and your fate will be a similar one."

Washington in the meantime had received a number of communications from General Clinton concerning the case of Major André. Clinton, Arnold and Robinson conferred together as to the means of obtaining the release of André. Arnold wrote a letter to Clinton assuming the responsibility for André's conduct, declaring that he came to him under the protection of a flag of truce, and that he gave him passports to go to White Plains on his return to New York. This impertinent letter from the traitor, enclosed in one from himself, Clinton forwarded to Washington, claiming that André should be permitted to return to New York.

As might be expected, these letters had no influence upon the action of Washington. He referred the case of the prisoner to a board of general officers, which he ordered to meet on the 29th of September, 1780, and directed that after a careful examination this board should report their opinion " of the light in which Major André should be considered and the punishment that ought to be inflicted." This board consisted of six major generals and eight brigadier generals, who went into the case with unusual care.

When Major André was brought before the board of officers he met with every indulgence, and was requested to answer no questions which would even embarrass his feelings. He frankly confessed all the facts relating to himself. Indeed, the facts were not controverted, and the board reported that André ought to be considered as a spy, and, agreeable to the usages of nations, must suffer death. André met the result with manly firmness.

" I foresaw my fate," said he, " and though I do not pretend to play the hero or to be indifferent about life, yet I am reconciled to whatever may happen, conscious that misfortune and not guilt has brought it upon me."

The execution was to have taken place on the 1st of October at five o'clock in the evening, but Washington received a second letter from Clinton expressing the opinion that the board had not been rightly informed of all the circumstances on which a judgment ought to be formed and adding, " I think it of the highest moment to humanity that your Excellency should be perfectly appraised of the state of this matter before you proceed to put that judgment into execution."

Accordingly he sent three of his staff officers to give

Washington, as he declared, the true state of the facts. These gentlemen came accompanied by Colonel Beverly Robinson. General Greene on the part of Washington met the party and after a long conference left to report to Washington all that had been urged in behalf of André. Later General Greene sent a note to Colonel Robinson informing him that he had made as full a report of their conference as his memory would permit, but that it had made no alteration in the opinion and determination of Washington.

André died possessing the sympathy of his judges and the friendship of all the American officers with whom he had been brought into familiar intercourse. Both Tallmadge and Hamilton expressed for him an attachment almost passionate. He died in the full uniform of his rank in the British army. A letter from André to Sir Henry Clinton expressed gratitude for his kindness and commended to his consideration his mother and sister and excusing his commander from all responsibility for his fate, saying among other things, " I have obtained General Washington's permission to send you this letter, the object of which is to remove from your breast any suspicion that I should imagine that I was bound by your Excellency's orders to expose myself to what has happened. The events of coming within an enemy's lines and of changing my dress, which led me to my present situation, were contrary to my own intentions as they were to your orders, and the circuitous route upon which I took to return was pressed, perhaps unavoidably and without alternative, upon me. I am perfectly tranquil in mind and prepared for any fate to which an honest zeal for my king's service may have conducted me."

On the 10th of August, 1821, the remains of André were removed from the banks of the Hudson to Westminster Abbey and interred there near the monument which had long been erected to his memory. In the south aisle near the window and surrounded by many great names is his monument on which is inscribed:

"Sacred to the memory of Major John André, who rose by his merits at an early period of life to the rank of Adjutant General of the British forces in America; and employed in an important but hazardous enterprise, fell a sacrifice to his zeal for his king and country, on the Second of October, 1780. Age 29. Universally beloved and esteemed by the army in which he served and lamented even by his foes.

"His Grace and Sovereign, King George III, has caused this monument to be erected."

It is an interesting fact that André never ceased in his affection for Honora Sneyd. He kept his pledge to be faithful to her always. His letters are full of the hopes and expectations of ambitious young manhood. While in New York with Sir Henry Clinton he was a great social favorite. Many proud young women, especially among the Tories, would have been glad of a matrimonial alliance with the handsome young aide-de-camp. André was human enough to appreciate and enjoy all of this flattery, but his heart was true to the girl he met in Litchfield. When the three farmers arrested him they stripped him — as they thought — of all he possessed, but he managed to keep the portrait of Miss Sneyd, which he always carried about his person, by concealing it in his mouth.   He thought of her to the last.

And the pathos of it all lay in the fact that he expired in ignorance of the fact that she had died in London, two months before.

VI

THE STRANGE ADVENTURES OF THE CHEVALIER D'EON AT THE RUSSIAN COURT

THE STRANGE ADVENTURES OF THE CHEVALIER D'EON AT THE RUSSIAN COURT

THE Chevalier D'Eon was not a military spy in the ordinary sense of the term, but his secret mission to the Russian Court, in the disguise of a woman, was the direct means of reëstablishing diplomatic relations between Russia and France and of preventing England from obtaining the services of 60,000 Russian soldiers to be used whenever the emergency might require them.

Charles Genevieve Louis Auguste Andre Timothee D'Eon de Beaumont was the full name of this curious character who took part in one of the most remarkable adventures in the history of war, politics or diplomacy.

Before he appeared on the scene Chancellor Bestuzhev of the Russian Ministry and the English and Austrian Ambassadors had been engaged in a long and perplexing negotiation which was expected to end in a new treaty between Russia and England. His English Majesty, King George II, was haunted by the fear that France and Prussia had designs on Hanover. To prevent this he wished to make an alliance against these countries with Russia and Austria. Empress Elizabeth of Russia did not display much interest in the proposition, but her Chancellor, Bestuzhev, was eager to consummate the plan because he had no love for the King of Prussia and believed that any extensions of that monarch's kingdom would be detrimental to Russia.

Bestuzhev's scheme was to raise 60,000 recruits who were to be placed at the service of England in return for a subsidy which was placed at five hundred thousand pounds. This was in January, 1755; but between the desire of the English cabinet to reduce the amount of the subsidy and the indifference of the Russian Empress, the affair dragged along for many months. Indeed, the patience of the English ambassador — Guy Dickens — was so sorely tried that he resigned in a huff and was succeeded by Sir Charles Hanbury Williams, one of the most notable men of the period, who determined to distinguish himself by bringing about the alliance which his predecessor at St. Petersburg had failed to accomplish.

Lord Holderness, the English Foreign Secretary, gave the new Ambassador to Russia minute directions concerning what he was expected to do at St. Petersburg. In a letter dated April 11, 1755, he said among other things: "On this occasion it will be proper to convince the Russians that they will remain only an Asiatic power if they sit still and give the King of Prussia an opportunity of putting into execution his ambitious, dangerous and long-concerted schemes of aggrandizement. His Majesty has authorized you, by your full powers and instructions, to do what may be necessary for preventing such a calamity."

The new Ambassador went to work with great energy and if the private letters and memoirs of the time are to be credited he soon found that he was engaged in a most expensive undertaking. Nearly everybody about the Russian Court wanted money and wanted it badly. Ten thousand pounds, it is stated, besides " the usual diplomatic presents " were given to the Chancellor. " An extraordinary gift " was made to the Vice-Chancellor. After that the Secretary to the Cabinet had to be considered and a letter to London said that this person could be obtained " for fifteen hundred ducats ready money, and five hundred per annum pension." But the money grabbers did not end here, for the bribery continued all along the line.

As a climax to this wholesale palm greasing, a convention was signed on the 9th of August, 1755, the chief feature of which was that Russia's aid to England should extend to all the allies of King George and that on the first demand for help from England, Russia would march 30,000 men against Prussia. This arrangement was to be ratified two months from the date of signing, but in the meantime was not to be binding.

Such were the methods of diplomacy 160 years ago! Is it surprising that the word at that time should come to have a shady meaning?

But unexpectedly an obstacle arose. Louis XV of France wished to renew diplomatic intercourse with the Court of Elizabeth. The Empress was favorable to this but her ministers knew that if it were accomplished the new treaty with England would be " merely a scrap of paper " — that it would be consigned to the waste basket.

Every attempt on the part of the French authorities to communicate with her was frustrated.   Presently a Frenchman, the Chevalier de Valcroissant, appeared in St. Petersburg.   His mission was to ascertain the feelings of the Russian Court toward the French monarch. He found out sooner than he expected, and in a way he did not relish.   Charged with being a spy, he was arrested and shut in the fortress of Schlosselburg. Louis XV was furious but helpless.   France did not have the power to protest against this proceeding because Valcroissant was not an accredited agent; he had only been sent as a private emissary to get the lay of the land.

Louis XV was not the sort of a man to abandon an enterprise.   He considered how he could penetrate the barrier of diplomats and spies who were surrounding the Empress Elizabeth.   And suddenly he thought of the man to accomplish this seemingly impossible feat.

It was the Chevalier D'Eon.

This talented young man, who had written a pamphlet on the financial condition of France under Louis XIV, had gained the friendship of the king and was in the Secret Service of his country.   He had distinguished himself as a soldier at an early age, and was noted for the success with which he had performed several confidential missions.

It was decided that he should go to Russia with the Chevalier Douglass, and that he should go in female attire.   Douglass was to leave France quietly on the

THE CHEVALIER D'EON

pretext of traveling for his health and his supposed
woman companion was to be represented as his niece.
Above all he was not to have any communication with
any French officials whether in France or during the
course of his travels.

His instructions were given in great detail.   He was
to enter Germany though Sweden, and to pass into
Bohemia on the plea of examining its mines.   On
reaching St. Petersburg he was directed to make the
acquaintance of any persons who might be able to help
him in his enterprise.   Among other things he had
orders to ascertain the influence which was exerted over
Elizabeth by her favorites and to send this information
from time to time to Louis XV.   No letters were to be
posted in the ordinary way, but all negotiations were to
be reported by means of a cipher code which was to
be forwarded to private addresses in Paris.

The Chevalier D'Eon entered into the affair with
much enthusiasm.   His appearance easily lent itself to
the disguise of a female.   He was small and slight
and had a pink and white complexion and his expression was gentle.   A sweet voice helped to make his
disguise complete.   This exploit of the notorious
adventurer afterwards gave him an unwelcome fame
which he was never able to live down, although history
proves that he was a brave soldier and had many manly
qualifications.   His defense for the remarkable esca-
pade was love of country, a taste for adventure and the
fact that a spy must do many things that would be dis-
tasteful to a soldier.

Before D'Eon left Paris he was given a copy of a

French novel, which had concealed between the boards
of its binding a letter from Louis XV to the Empress
Elizabeth.   It also contained a cipher which the Empress and her Vice Chancellor Woronzoff were to use
in corresponding with the French king.   It is a significant fact that this volume never left the possession of
the young adventurer.   He read it on all occasions —
in his room at hotels and even while he waited for an
audience with the officials of the Russian Court.   Is it
any wonder that he gained the reputation of being an
omnivorous novel reader?

The little drama began when the Chevalier Douglass
arrived at Anhalt and stopped at one of the hotels to
await the arrival of his delightful niece.   She arrived
in due time, did Mademoiselle Lia de Beaumont, and
made an immediate and favorable impression on all
with whom she came in contact.   Such charm!   Such
shyness!   Such modesty and at the same time such
sprightliness!   Is it any wonder that Douglass and his
young relative at once gained the attention of the best
society of the place?   They were pressed to make a
long stay at Anhalt, but declined on the ground that it
was necessary to proceed to the capital.

In St. Petersburg they stayed at the house of Monsieur Michael, the French banker, who was a man of
eminence in the Russian city.   One of the first persons
to meet Douglass was the Austrian Ambassador.   He
was curious about the new arrivals.

" What are you doing in this country? " he asked.

The wily courier of the king was seized with a fit of
coughing and at its conclusion replied:

" I am here by the advice of my physician, in order to get the benefit of a cold climate."

All the while the real purposes of Chevalier Douglass were in microscopic characters on the sheet of thin paper concealed in the false bottom of a tortoise shell snuff box. Every time he took a pinch of snuff he thought of his mission. Also he was sure that if he should be suspected and searched that the snuff box would escape attention and confiscation. But as the days went by the charming niece was seized with a desire to see the Empress, not in a public, but in a private audience.

How was this to be accomplished?

The French banker who was acting as host to the queer couple was acquainted with the Vice Chancellor, who had no love for the Chancellor. So he invited the first named personage to his house to meet Douglass and his "adorable niece". The Vice Chancellor was delighted with the newcomers and readily agreed to present the niece privately to the Empress.

The meeting took place in one of the large rooms of the palace and as soon as they were alone the fascinating young woman exclaimed:

" Your Majesty, I am not what I seem. I am the Chevalier D'Eon sent to you as the special messenger of Louis XV. It was necessary to come to you in this guise to outwit your court officers who were determined that no message from the King should reach you."

At first amazed, the Empress afterwards felt flattered that such extraordinary means should be employed to obtain her attention, and she made the supposed female sit down and tell her the story of how the ruse had been planned and executed. After that D'Eon told of the desire of the King to resume diplomatic relations with the Russian Court. Her Majesty was greatly flattered. The manner in which she had been approached appealed to her imagination, and she agreed that the deception of her ministers should be continued. In order that the scheme might be facilitated, she appointed D'Eon her reader, which not only gave him a reason for being about the Court, but also furnished him with ready access to her at all times.

In a very short time she gave him a written statement in which she expressed a willingness to receive and to accord " respectful treatment for any envoy of the King of France who would bring with him sufficient powers to sign a treaty." With this precious paper in his posession Douglass hastened to Paris to give it to the King. D'Eon, in the meantime, remained in St. Petersburg in order to see that there were no unexpected developments that would militate against King Louis XV. There can be no doubt but that it was the secret influence which Douglass and D'Eon had with the Empress which led her to neglect the treaty with England which the Chancellor had fully expected her to sign.

" I am sorry to say," writes the English Ambassador to Lord Holderness, " that it is impossible for the Chancellor to get her Majesty to put her signature to the treaty which we so much desire. He appears to be very much in awe of her." Little did the diplomats suspect that their carefully laid plans had been upset by the " charming niece " of the Chevalier Douglass.

In the meantime other events were occurring in other parts of the world which served to make still further impossible the thing which England had so ardently desired. King George had become alarmed over the unexpected delay and entered into a defensive alliance with the King of Prussia. By this the Prussian monarch agreed to defend Hanover. This treaty was signed at Westminster on January 16, 1756. The news was sent to the English Ambassador at St. Petersburg, who promptly communicated it to the Chancellor Bestuzhev.

That aged, if not venerable, diplomat swore violently. And little wonder, for it meant that his long-sought scheme to humiliate Frederick of Prussia and to gain England as an ally, had collapsed. After he had partially recovered his self-possession he exclaimed:

" This union between England and Prussia will be bitter news to her Imperial Majesty."

" Why so? " replied the innocent English Ambassador. " Such an alliance can offend no one but France."

In the meantime the treaty between England and Russia was still regarded as a desirable thing and Bestuzhev and the English Ambassador worked hard with that end in view.

The hint was given that some financial gifts promised by England had not arrived, but the English Ambassador assured the Russian Chancellor that it would all be received in due time and that if necessary the

promised sums would be advanced at once.   As a consequence of this there was much activity about the Russian Court.   Finally the long deferred ratification took
place on February 4, 1756, but there had been slyly
added to the treaty a phrase stating that it would be
valid only in case the King of Prussia attacked the
dominions of his Majesty, the King of Great Britain.
The English Ambassador strongly protested against
this clause because it made his labor of many months
and his splendid financial " gifts " practically useless,
but he was obliged to accept the paper as it stood.

But the worst was still to come.   When the Empress
became fully informed of the treaty between Prussia
and England she was furious, and immediately declared that the arrangement just made between her
own country and England should be declared void.
Bestuzhev was frantic at this order which destroyed
the work which had cost him so much time and labor.
Indeed, so far did he go that the Empress reprimanded
him for his impertinence.

The changed condition of diplomatic relations in the
world now made it more desirable than ever that
France should be represented at the Russian Court.
The Chevalier Douglass was sent by Louis XV to St.
Petersburg for the second time.   He reached there in
April, 1756, and was so eager to present himself that
late on the evening of his arrival he called on the Vice
Chancellor and handed him a letter from the French
King to the Russian Empress.   The Vice Chancellor,
who was in sympathy with the program of the French,
made it a point to present the messenger from Paris to

the Empress that very night. Elizabeth was not very well pleased that the Chevalier Douglass should be sent to her Court as an unofficial agent instead of an accredited minister, but in spite of this fact she received him graciously and listened to what he had to say. A few days later she sent for Douglass and gave him a note addressed to the French Minister of Foreign Affairs in which it was stated that it would be agreeable to her Imperial Majesty if the Chevalier Douglass was more fully authorized or accredited as chargé d'affaires, so that it would be possible for both sides to treat with greater authority on the matters included in his instructions. She added that this would not only be to the mutual advantage of both courts but would also tend to hasten their reunion in a diplomatic sense. It was further stated that notwithstanding the failure to make the Chevalier Douglass an accredited minister he would be treated with distinction and listened to with great consideration as being a person sent to Russia on the part of Louis XV.

Shortly before this meeting between the Empress and Douglass, the Chevalier D'Eon had returned to Paris, but during his stay in St. Petersburg he had won the friendship and favor of the Empress. He had on numerous occasions acted as her reader and his great knowledge of men and things in all parts of the world had furnished her with more than ordinary entertainment. She learned that he had a real knowledge of art and literature and also that while living in Paris he had been in the midst of many men distinguished in literature, politics and art. Also she had him recount to her his early experiences as the son of a Tonnere lawyer and the descendant of a good family. D'Eon was not the sort of a person to boast of his personal courage, but by close questioning she learned that he had been engaged in many military exploits which redounded to his credit.

As a result of all this she desired very much that the Chevaliers Douglass and D'Eon should be returned to her court as thoroughly accredited representatives of their Government, but while she was working to this end, her Chancellor and the English Ambassador were doing all in their power to prevent the consummation desired by the French king. Indeed, the English representative still had hopes of accomplishing the task he had been instructed to perform. His only fear seems to have been that the health of the Empress, which was not very good at that time, might become worse and leave the matter suspended, like Mohammed's coffin, between Heaven and earth. The Court was in what might be described as a state of uproar, and Sir Charles Williams, writing to Lord Holderness, says: "The state of the Empress's health has been extremely bad. On the 16th instant there was a ball at Court, and after the Imperial Ambassador of Austria was gone she told me she would dance a minuet with me. As soon as it was over she was so spent that she retired into her own apartments for a quarter of an hour. She then returned into the ballroom and taking me aside told me in a very affecting strain how ill she was. She said that her cough had lasted nine minutes and she could not get rid of it, and that she had quite lost her appetite. While she was telling me this she was seized with another fit of coughing that obliged her to retire, and she appeared no more."

In another letter addressed to his superior, Sir Charles says: "Last night the Empress was much worse. She intends if possible, however, going to Count Esterhasy's ball, which he gives in honor of the young grand duke next Wednesday, and there is actually a machine making to carry her Majesty from one floor to another without obliging her to mount the stairs. I leave your Lordship to imagine the alarm which this Court it in. I had much conversation last night with the Grand Chancellor on the present scene. He perhaps is less alarmed than other people, for the Grand Duchess is his friend and is governed by him. As her Imperial Highness is the person who in case of accidents will rule here, I think it will be well to inform the King of my observations upon her, which I can the better do because I often have conversations with her for long periods, as my rank places me at supper always next to Her Imperial Highness, and almost from the beginning of my being here she has treated me with confidence, and sent word by the Grand Chancellor that she would do so."

But all of the solicitude of the English Ambassador was lost. He could not get the Empress to agree to the reopening of negotiations looking to the treaty between the two countries. On the contrary she renewed her request to King Louis XV for an official representation of that country at the Russian Court. The Empress's request was given prompt consideration, for in July of the same year the Chevalier Douglass was accredited chargé d'affaires to the Russian Court, while D'Eon, the dashing young adventurer, joined him, no longer in woman's apparel but in the handsome dress of a fashionable young man. He was appointed and served with great success as Secretary of the French Legation at the Russian Court. It is very significant of the waning influence of the wily Chancellor in the esteem of the Empress, that he knew nothing of the arrangement by which Douglass and D'Eon were sent to St. Petersburg until these two persons had reached the frontier town of Riga.

This was an instance where French shrewdness got the better of English gold. Chancellor Bestuzhev was outwitted and outplayed at every stage of the diplomatic game. He realized, when it was too late, that he had been beaten by a French spy, disguised as a woman, and the recollection of it embittered the remainder of his life.

There was a dramatic sequel to this defeat, which fortunately for those concerned, did not have a fatal ending. Armed thugs entered the house where Douglass and D'Eon were sleeping and, rushing into the room, fired several shots at the young men.

They escaped with their lives and were content to regard the affair as an ordinary case of housebreaking. But if either of them had been called upon to point the finger of suspicion at any one, it would have been straight in the direction of Chancellor Bestuzhev.

HOW NAPOLEON'S CHIEF SPY
HOODWINKED THE EMPEROR
OF AUSTRIA

HOW NAPOLEON'S CHIEF SPY HOODWINKED THE EMPEROR OF AUSTRIA

THE amazing audacity of Charles Louis Schulmeister — Napoleon's chief spy — was never illustrated to better advantage than when he hoodwinked Francis II, Emperor of Austria.

The episode really had its inception on the twenty-third of October, 1805, when Napoleon sent for his favorite and told him that he wanted to know the plans of the Austrian army. At that time General Kontovsoff was believed to be hurrying westward with 60,000 Russians. It was characteristic of Schulmeister that he received this commission as a matter of course. He had men and money at his disposal and was in a position to command the attention of the great. But his biggest asset was his fearlessness.

On the day after his interview with Napoleon he started on the mission which was to involve him in the most sensational events of his checkered career. He met his old friend and confederate, Lieutenant Bendel, at Muhldorf, and by him was presented to General Kienmayer, in command of the Austrian forces. He was well received as before by this officer, who regarded him as a member of the Austrian Secret Ser-

vice. Indeed, Kienmayer had taken a liking to the
medium-sized man with the scarred forehead and was
glad to meet him again. He little thought that this
was the man who had betrayed the Austrian military
secrets and who, more than any one individual, was
responsible for the maneuvers which had resulted in
the surrender of Field Marshal Mack.

Schulmeister, with his unwavering blue eyes and his
brusque soldierly manner, had several talks with Kienmayer and learned that the Austrian was not yet ready
to take the offensive. Also he was given an inkling of
the movements of General Kontovsoff. This valuable
information was transmitted to Napoleon, who made
his plans accordingly.

But Schulmeister was not satisfied to stop at this
stage of the game. He had another scheme hatching
in his fertile mind, and presently he made it known to
his friend Bendel.

"I want you to get me permission to wear the uniform of an Austrian staff officer."

Bendel, who had already gone to great lengths to
serve the spy, gasped at the daring of this latest request.

"But why?" he asked. "What reason can be given
for such a thing?"

The blue-eyed one smiled grimly. The humor of
the business was not lost on him.

"The best reason in the world," he replied. "It is
but a slight return for all I have done for the Austrian
army."

The things he had done for the Austrian army, had
they been known to Kienmayer, would have caused

that officer to give an order for Schulmeister's execution at sunrise. Instead of that he gave him permission to wear the Austrian uniform. The result of this was far-reaching. It helped to make history. In a word, it placed the Austrian army — or a considerable section of it — at the mercy of the Alsatian smuggler.

Schulmeister went to Vienna, where he proclaimed himself to be the representative of General Kienmayer. Vienna, even at that time, was numbered among the gayest capitals of Europe, and the supposed secret service agent of the Austrian commander was received with open arms and treated with marked distinction. He mingled with the officers and was entertained at the cafés and altogether made a marked impression with the people. His natural qualities helped him greatly in this bold adventure. The scars on his forehead, his apparent reticence and his military bearing all helped to win the confidence of those with whom he was thrown into contact.

The Emperor Francis II was in Vienna at the time, and Schulmeister was told that he would have an opportunity of meeting him in person. He did not shrink from the ordeal. Indeed, he may be said to have courted it. The Emperor at that time had reached a critical stage of his career. He came into power at a time when the French revolution was exciting the alarm of most of the old European dynasties. Austria was in alliance with Prussia against the advances of the new republic. In 1795–96, the war between France and Austria raged fiercely on German soil. In 1796 Napoleon, whose meteoric career was astonishing the

world, swept through northern Italy and the next year
invaded Austria.   As a consequence of this, Francis
was compelled to sign the treaty of Campo Formio, by
which Austria surrendered Belgium and Lombardy,
receiving in return most of the dominions of the extinct
Republic of Venice.   Smarting under this, Francis,
two years later, made an alliance with Russia and
England.   Again he took up arms and at the outset
met with a number of successes.

But the recall of the Russian general Suvaroff and
the return of Napoleon from the East, turned the tide
against him.   The victories won by Bonaparte at Ma-
rengo and by Morean at Hohenlinden seriously crippled
the power of Austria, and Francis was reduced to the
necessity of suing for peace.   By the treaty of Luné-
ville in 1801, France was confirmed in the possession
of the left bank of the Rhine.   In 1804 Francis
assumed the title of the Emperor of Austria, and in
the following year entered into a new alliance with
Russia.   The following year began the contest with
Napoleon which was to end so disastrously for the
Austrians.   This was the condition of affairs that
existed when Napoleon's chief spy found himself in
the Austrian capital, clothed in the uniform of an Austrian officer.

He had not been there long before he learned that a
most important council of war was to be held, at which
plans were to be matured for the purpose of checking
the aggressions of Napoleon.   He resolved to attend
that council.   As before, he had the aid of Lieutenant
Bendel.   It was by means of this officer that he was

taken into the confidence of the Secretary of the Council and told that he would be admitted to its deliberations. A less audacious man would have hesitated to attend such a meeting. Even Bendel warned him of the danger he ran.

" You are putting your head into the lion's mouth," said he.

" It doesn't matter," he retorted; " the animal has no teeth."

At the appointed hour Schulmeister presented himself at the palace, and presenting the proper credentials, was admitted. An orderly conducted him along narrow passages and up a flight of stairs to a wide corridor which led to the conference chamber. Lieutenant Bendel had preceded him there and at three knocks on the door he was ushered into the room. It was a long, high-ceilinged apartment with a raised dais at the far end.

It was evident, at a glance, that this was used as a sort of war office. Large maps were spread out on the walls and a globe stood in the center of the apartment. Colored pins were stuck into the maps to indicate the positions of the various armies then in the field.

A number of officers were present and others continued to come until probably fifteen men were in the room. Schulmeister was presented to them by Lieutenant Bendel, and was greeted, for the most part, in a perfunctory manner. The pride-stricken members had very little time to give to one who appeared to be below them in rank. One or two, attracted by the report that

the newcomer was a member of the Austrian Secret
Service, paused long enough to ask him a few questions concerning the character of his work.   He replied
in a way that satisfied them without committing himself.   Schulmeister was at his best in situations of
this kind.   His natural reticence served him well.
Somehow he gave one the impression of imparting a
great deal of information in a very few words.

At all events he was fortunate in being lost amid the
titled and gold lace of the occasion.   A large table was
placed in front of the raised dais at the end of the room
and the conferees drew up chairs and began a general
conversation.   The Alsatian spy managed to keep in
the background and yet to be in a position to see and to
hear all that was taking place.   In the midst of the
talk there was a flutter at the entrance to the apartment
and an official voice called out:

" Gentlemen, the King! "

Everybody arose and stood at attention while Francis II rapidly walked down the center of the room and
took his place in the big chair on the raised platform.
As he sat down the others resumed their places.   The
monarch looked worn and worried and he proceeded to
the business in hand in a listless sort of style.   Schulmeister, to his relief, was not even noticed by the monarch, who was plainly preoccupied.

For three quarters of an hour the members of the
council of war discussed their plans while the spy of
Napoleon drank in every word.   It was a situation
without a parallel, probably, in the history of warfare.
Spies have found their way into the councils of the

enemy, but there is no other case on record where the
sovereign of a great empire has openly discussed his
plans before a spy from the opposing army.   Presently
the affair came to an end and Schulmeister left with
the others.   He gave a sigh of satisfaction as he
breathed the free air again and before an hour passed
had sent an account of the proceedings to Napoleon.

Some one must have detected him in the act of relay-
ing his messages — because he had a system of his
own of getting his information through the lines — for
he began to be regarded with suspicion.   He carried
himself with great calmness but he was too adept in the
art of spying not to know that he was being shadowed.
Everywhere that he went he was followed by Austrian
officers.   Evidently they were not sure of their man.
He was suspected, but the proof was wanting.   He
thought he might wear out the patience of his shad-
owers, but he was mistaken in this.

Finally the situation became so acute that he resolved
to fly for his life.   He left in the middle of the night
and managed to reach Moravia.   Here a burly Austrian staff officer pulled him out of bed without any
ceremony.

" You are wanted in Vienna," he said gruffly.

" But I have been there," protested Schulmeister;
" and now it is most important that I should proceed
on my way."

The officer roared with laughter.

" I don't doubt it, but we wish to show you some
attention at the capital."

Schulmeister made a final effort.   He produced the

letters by which he had wormed his way into the good graces of the Secretary of the Council.

"Here are my credentials. What more do you wish?"

"Nothing," roared the big fellow, as he grabbed the letters. "These are what we have been hunting. They will be put to the test and you will come and answer to the charge of being a spy."

This was a truly alarming situation, but the Alsatian smuggler carried himself with great confidence and dignity. In his heart of hearts he felt that he was lost. His wonderful activity had made him known to many persons and surely some of them would appear against him.

The court martial which was called to consider the case of Schulmeister met in Vienna and was surrounded with great pomp and dignity. The soldierly appearance of the accused and his refusal to defend himself aroused a great deal of sympathy in his case. But the weight of the evidence was against him. It was proven that he had given false information to General Mack in the Ulm campaign and it was shown that he had been in Vienna under false pretenses. After due deliberations the verdict was rendered and it condemned him to death as a spy.

Schulmeister fought for time to the last. He believed that something might happen to relieve him from his dangerous position. The general in command directed that he should be shot at sunrise. The Alsatian betrayed no emotion when he heard the dreadful words. Indeed, danger had become so great a part of

his everyday life that it had no terrors for him. Death
·in any form did not shock him — not even when it was
to be his own. He called for pen, ink and paper and
spent a long time writing in his cell. It has been said
that he scribbled reports which he hoped to have smug-
gled into the French lines. If this be true it.proves
that Schulmeister was as much patriot as spy. But
the story rests on tradition, and, of course, is impossible of verification, by means of documentary evidence.

After that he waited for morning. To the ordinary
man this would have seemed a long black night, but
there is nothing to indicate that it caused the Alsatian
any great mental anguish. His mind was busy turning
over the possibility of escape, but otherwise he was
placid and self-contained. He simply sat there on his
low wooden stool and watched for the sunrise that was
to be the signal for his execution.

While Schulmeister was going through this thrilling
experience Napoleon was hammering at the gates of
Vienna. He had pursued the armies of Russia and
Austria from one point to another, all the time working to accomplish his favorite maxim, "Divide in
order to subsist; concentrate in order to fight." As
the contest went along the ardor of the Russian army
grew more intense. It advanced toward the position
long studied by Napoleon and which he destined for
his field of battle. We are told by the historian Guizot
that in accordance with the plan of the Austrian general Weirother, the allies had resolved to turn the
right of the French army in order to cut off the road

to Vienna by assaulting the numerous corps dispersed in Austria and Styria. Altogether, the two emperors and their staff officers occupied the castle and village of Austerlitz. On the first of December, 1805, the allies established themselves upon the plateau Platzen. Napoleon by design had left this free, divining with a sure instinct of superior genius the maneuvers of the enemy he had cleverly drawn into the snare. His proclamation to the troops announced the plan of the battle.

"Soldiers," said he, "the Russian army presents itself before you to avenge the Austrian army of Ulm. These are the same battalions you have beaten at Hollabrunn and that you have constantly pursued to this place. The positions that we occupy are formidable and whilst they march to turn my right they will present me their flank.

"Soldiers, I will myself direct your battalions. I will keep myself away from the firing if with your accustomed bravery you carry disorder and confusion into the enemy's ranks. But if the victory were for a moment uncertain you would see your emperor expose himself to the brunt of the attack; for this victory will finish the campaign and we shall be able to resume our winter quarters where we shall be joined by new armies which are forming in France. Then the peace I shall make will be worthy of my people, of you, and of me."

It so happened that this was the eve of the anniversary of the coronation of the Emperor. The soldiers in order to celebrate the event gathered up the straw upon which they were stretched and, making it into bundles, they lit them at the end of poles.

"Be assured," said an old grenadier, advancing toward the chief who had so many times led his comrades to victory, "that we will bring thee to-morrow the flags and cannon of the Russian army to signalize the anniversary of the Second of December."

The fires were extinguished and the Austrians thought they saw in this the indication of a night retreat. Gathered around the map, the allied generals listened to Weirother, who developed his plan of battle with a boasting air which displayed in him a clear persuasion of his own merits. He said to his associates:

"We do not think him strong. If he has 40,000 men it is all. He is extinguishing his fires and a good deal of noise is coming from his camp. He is either retreating or else he is changing his position."

At daylight the next morning the battle began. It was one of the fiercest in all of the Napoleonic wars. Murat and Lanes attacked on the left eighty-two Russian and Austrian squadrons under the orders of Prince John of Lichtenstein. General Valhubert had his thigh fractured and the soldiers wished to carry him away.

"Remain at your posts," said he calmly. "I know well how to die alone. We must not for one man lose six."

Finally the tide, which comes in every great battle, turned in favor of the French. General Doctoroff and Kienmayer effected a painful retreat, under the

fire of the French batteries, by a narrow embankment
separating the two lakes of Melintz and Falnitz.   The
awful day came to a close with French shouts of victory.

Napoleon, as was customary, harangued his army.

"Soldiers," said he, "I am satisfied with you.
You have justified all that I expected from you.   An
army of 100,000 men commanded by the Emperors of
Russia and Austria has been in less than four hours
either cut up or dispersed, and what escaped from your
steel is drowned in the lakes.   Forty flags or standards
of the Imperial Guard of Russia, 120 pieces of cannon,
20 generals and more than 30,000 prisoners are the
results of this ever memorable day.   In three months
this third coalition has been vanquished and dissolved.
Soldiers, when all that is necessary in order to assure
the happiness and prosperity of France shall be accomplished, I will lead you back into France.   There you
will be the object of my most tender solicitude."

Prior to this the French troops had pressed on into
Vienna.   A detachment hurried to the prison where
Charles Louis Schulmeister was awaiting his execution.   They arrived in the nick of time and released
him from what seemed to be certain death.   He was
calmer and more collected than any one in the crowd.

"Frenchmen," he cried, with a mixture of irony and
joy, "I greet you.   I welcome you to the City of
Vienna."

Schulmeister was naturally one of the heroes of the
day and when Napoleon went to meet the Emperor
Francis on the following day he formed one of the

small bodyguard that accompanied the great soldier. The conference between the two crowned heads took place at the mill of Paleny, between Nasiedlowitz and Urschitz. The spy kept in the background and was not observed by the vanquished monarch.

Napoleon treated his fallen foe with great courtesy and made excuses for the poor place in which he was compelled, to receive Francis II.

" These are the palaces," said he, " which Your Majesty has compelled me to inhabit for the last three months."

" Your visit has succeeded sufficiently well for you to have no right to bear me any grudge," replied the Austrian Emperor.

The two monarchs embraced and the armistice was concluded. A formal order from Napoleon was necessary in order to stop the march of Marshal Davont, who was in pursuit of the Russian army. General Savery, the friend of Schulmeister, was entrusted with this order. He carried to the Czar the conditions of the armistice.

" I am satisfied, since my ally is," replied Alexander, and he allowed to escape from him the expression of admiration which he could not restrain. " Your master," he said, " has shown himself to be very great."

After more weighty matters had been settled Napoleon sent for Schulmeister and congratulated him upon his courage and level-headedness.

" As a mark of my confidence," he said, " I make you chief of police of Vienna."

It was a rich plum — in its way one of the richest

at the disposal of the Emperor.   The smuggler of the Alsatian village was a man who knew how to adapt himself to circumstances.   In his new post he displayed great executive ability, and if he added to his fortune — well, those were the times when it was declared unblushingly that " to the victors belong the spoils."

VIII

LYDIA DARRAH, THE BRAVE QUAKERESS
WHO SAVED WASHINGTON'S ARMY
FROM DESTRUCTION

VIII

LYDIA DARRAH, THE BRAVE QUAKERESS
WHO SAVED WASHINGTON'S ARMY
FROM DESTRUCTION

WHILE the British occupied Philadelphia during the Revolutionary War most of their
time was given to the pleasures of life. It
was this fact that caused Franklin to observe with
characteristic shrewdness that " Howe had not taken
Philadelphia but Philadelphia had taken Howe."
There was, however, one serious attempt made to destroy Washington's army during the period and, curiously enough, it was frustrated by the courage, the
wit and the promptness of a brave Quakeress.

When the British took possession of the city the
officers appropriated the most desirable dwellings for
their headquarters. Thus General Harris practically
confiscated the home of General Cadwallader, on Second Street, four doors below Spruce. Directly opposite this, on the corner of Little Dock Street, was the
quaint home of William and Lydia Darrah, who were
members of the Society of Friends, whose members,
it need scarcely be said, have a profound repugnance
to war.

By one of those little ironies which constantly mock

our lives, the Adjutant-General of the British army
decided to make his home with the Darrahs. By the
polite fiction which sometimes prevails in time of war
as well as of peace, both pretended to be delighted with
the arrangement. It is certain that the Englishman
found a desirable and well kept colonial home for his
temporary habitation, while the Darrahs soon discovered that whatever else he might be, their war guest
was a gentleman.

Lydia Darrah had the reputation of being a Whig,
and she gloried in it. She made no secret of her feelings to her lodger, and one day when he reproached
her with her want of loyalty to the mother country,
she exclaimed with spirit:

"I hope thee is beaten — thee deserve to be for
coming across the ocean to subdue a liberty-loving
people."

He laughed at this outburst and remarked:

"I was beginning to flatter myself that you and
your husband looked upon me as a friend."

"And so we do. We detest the sin while pitying
the sinner. Though we consider thee as a public
enemy, we regard thee as a private friend. While we
detest the cause thee fights for, we wish well to thy
personal interest and safety."

"Oh!" he cried, jovially. "That sounds better.
You are really a friend of the King."

"Thee must not feel flattered," she said gravely.
"We are for the Colonists. Thee knows that every
unnecessary expense has been retrenched in this house.
Tea has not been drunk since last Christmas. Nor

have I bought a new cap or gown since your defeat
at Lexington.   Be assured that such is the feeling of
American women."

The Adjutant-General could not but admire the
spirit of such a woman.   Whatever else she might be
she was not deceitful.   She did not attempt to curry
favor with the British.   It rather pleased him to permit her to indulge in what might be considered treasonable sentiments.   No matter how radical might be her
views there could be no danger from this sweet-faced
little woman with the poke bonnet and the drab dress.
And, moreover, even when most spirited, there was no
bitterness or vindictiveness in her tone or manner.
As he gazed at her he felt that the serenity of her
countenance was truly an outward sign of the tran-
quillity of her life.

Among other things, the Adjutant-General had arranged for a room on the first floor to be used as a
sort of conference chamber for the British officers.
Here groups of the leading redcoats were wont to
assemble, by candle-light, for the purpose of discuss-
ing plans of campaigns.   Several of these gatherings
had been held without attracting any particular attention from Lydia Darrah.

Early in December, 1777, there was a strange halt
in the round of pleasure among the British officers in
Philadelphia.   The men were drilled and organized
as if in anticipation of a coming movement.   The indifference and indolence of the previous months gave
way to activity all along the line.   Lydia, who was a
true patriot, observed these signs with genuine distress.

She could not but feel that it boded ill to her country-men.

It was on the 2nd of December that the Adjutant-General sent for her. She noticed that he was serious and preoccupied.

" I wish to tell you," he said, " that we will require the use of the sitting-room at seven o'clock this evening. We may remain late and it is important that we should not be disturbed. For this reason I would ask you to have all of the members of your family retire early. When we are through and it is time for us to leave I will call you so that you may let us out. Do you understand? "

" Perfectly," she replied, with downcast eyes. " I will see that everything is prepared, and after that shall retire and wait until thee summons me."

On the night in question she carried out all of the orders with literal exactness. But she could not rest. The words of the British officer had filled her with curiosity and uneasiness. What did it mean? What was the object of this mysterious conference? Finally she could remain in her room no longer. She crept silently downstairs in her stockinged feet and took up a position outside of the door where the officers were assembled. By pressing her ear close to the crevices of the panels she could hear the talk from within. The words " Washington " and " Whitemarsh " attracted her attention and presently she obtained a connected story of their plans.

She was shocked, and with reason. What she had heard was an order for all the British troops to march

out on the evening of the fourth to attack the army of
General Washington, then encamped at Whitemarsh.
She knew what that would mean only too well.   Taken
unawares by superior numbers, the patriot army would
be destroyed.   And that destruction meant that the
torch of liberty would be extinguished — the hope of
freedom would be destroyed.

Lydia Darrah crept silently upstairs again and went
to bed, but not to sleep.   She was depressed and dis-
heartened.   The thought that the lives of Americans
might be lost in vain was intolerable.   And while the
members of her family slept soundly, and the officers
in the room below perfected their plans, she wondered
what could be done to avert the threatened calamity.

While her mind was filled with conflicting thoughts
there came a rap at her door and the voice of the Adjutant-General saying that they were ready to leave.
She remained perfectly quiet and then he knocked a
second time and louder than before.   Still no answer
and this time he pounded with his fists.   She arose,
and taking her time to dress, appeared at the door,
candle in hand, and pretended to be very drowsy.   He
apologized for having aroused her from sleep and left
the house with his companions.

From that moment she was so agitated that she could
neither sleep nor eat.   The question was how to get
the information to General Washington.   She dare not
confide in any one — not even her husband.   She decided to go to Whitemarsh herself.   In order to furnish a plausible excuse she informed the members of

her family that it was necessary to get a sack of flour from the mill at Frankford. Her husband protested.

" Send one of the servants," he said. " There is no good reason why thee should make such a long trip."

" No," she replied resolutely. " I shall go myself."

" But at least," he pleaded, " take one of the servant maids with thee."

" I shall go alone," she insisted with a determination that surprised and conquered him.

William Darrah learned on that occasion that a Quakeress, though placid in appearance, can be quite as obstinate as other members of her sex. He gazed wonderingly at the poke-bonneted woman as she left the house and started in the direction of General Howe's headquarters in order to get the requisite pass to get through the British lines.

General Howe received her kindly, if not almost jovially. He knew that the Adjutant-General of his army was quartered at the Darrah home, and he looked on Lydia as an interesting but harmless rebel. He was surrounded by members of his staff and they, like their superior, were disposed to jest with the Quakeress. But finally the coveted pasteboard was handed to her.

" Don't stay long," he smiled. " Your British guests will miss you."

The moment she received the pass she hurried away and once out of sight of the general's headquarters she almost ran until she reached Frankford. She left her bag at the mill, and saying she would return for it in a little while, continued her journey to Whitemarsh.

Washington had camped at this place after resting
for a few days at Perkiomen Creek.   He was reënforced by 1200 Rhode Island troops from Peekskill,
under General Varnum, and nearly 1000 Virginia,
Maryland and Pennsylvania soldiers.   He was now
within fourteen miles of Philadelphia.   By a resolution
of, Congress all persons taken within thirty miles of
any place occupied by the British troops, in the act of
conveying supplies to them, were subjected to martial
law.   Acting under the resolution, Washington detached large bodies of militia to scour the roads above
the city, and between the Schuylkill and Chester, to
intercept all supplies going to the enemy.

This served a double purpose.   It harassed Howe by
preventing him from receiving the supplies and gave
them to the Continentals.   All this time Washington was observing a prudent policy.   He was anxious
to fight, but he was only willing to do so under circumstances that would be advantageous to himself.   He
had many critics of this policy, and some of them said
nasty things, but Washington held steadily to his purpose in spite of good and evil reports.

Lydia Darrah plodded along to Whitemarsh, oblivious alike of the inclemency of the weather and her
personal discomfort.   Her one thought was to get the
warning to Washington, for whom she had a respect
and reverence that bordered on veneration.   After
leaving the mill at Frankford she encountered but few
persons, and these looked upon the little Quakeress
with only a listless curiosity.

It was when she had almost reached her destination

that she began to feel footsore and weary. She was filled with a great desire to sit by the roadside and rest, but she resisted the natural inclination and kept on to the end. Within that frail body and beneath those modest and peaceful garments there was a grim determination that was Spartan-like in its persistence and its ignoring of pain and suffering.

Just before she reached her goal she saw a mounted Continental officer. His back was turned to her and she debated the advisability of speaking to him. Before she reached a conclusion he had twisted about in his saddle and looked in her direction. The recognition was mutual. He was a young American officer of her acquaintance, Lieutenant Colonel Craig of the light horse. He was evidently amazed at seeing her in such a place, and, riding over, touched his hat.

"Have you lost your way?" he asked, and before she could answer he added, "and how did you get through the British lines?"

She smiled sweetly in spite of her fatigue.

"I came to get flour at the mill in Frankford. General Howe was good enough to give me a pass."

"But you are beyond Frankford," he protested.

"Perhaps," she said hesitatingly, "I may be in search of my son who is an officer in the American army."

"Perhaps," retorted Lieutenant Colonel Craig, doubtfully.

By this time several soldiers on foot came in the direction of the speakers. Lydia became nervous and ill at ease. She plucked at his coat.

LYDIA DARRAH AND LIEUTENANT-COLONEL CRAIG

"Dismount and walk aside with me," she whispered. "I have something to tell you."

He complied with her request, wonderingly. The Lieutenant Colonel and his companions constituted a squad that had been sent out by Washington to watch the roads and to gather information concerning the enemy. Little did he suspect that such important news was at hand. They walked some yards from the soldiers.

"Now," he commanded, "tell me what in the world you are doing so far from home."

"Lieutenant," she cried in a voice that trembled in spite of herself, "I came to warn General Washington that General Howe intends to attack the Continental army. He hopes to find General Washington unprepared."

"How do you know this?"

"I overheard it last night. The Adjutant-General and other officers met at my house to make their plans. I felt that General Washington must be warned and I walked here for that purpose."

The eyes of the young officer almost stared out of their sockets. He gazed down at the frail woman in amazement and admiration.

"Shall I take you to the General?"

"No, it is sufficient for you to know. It shall be your duty to tell him. And you must agree not to reveal your source of information. If it was known that I came here it would go hard with me — it might mean my death."

"I promise!" he said, solemnly.

Then and there the Quakeress told him all that had taken place in her house at the conference among the British officers. She had an excellent memory and was able to give him all the details of the proposed attack. As she concluded she said:

"You must not reveal my identity — even to your men."

"It shall be as you wish, and now you must rest and have food."

She protested feebly, but he was not to be gainsaid, and insisted upon escorting her to a nearby farmhouse where she might obtain food and also rest for a while before taking the long walk back to the city. She urged him to go to Washington at once, saying the message he had to convey was more important than her personal comfort. But he was a gentleman as well as a patriot and he did not leave her until she had been safely housed and her wants attended to. On leaving he stooped and kissed her hand.

"You have saved the army," he said, "and you will not be forgotten as long as liberty endures."

She did not stay long, and, after a light meal, left for the return to Philadelphia. She paused at Frankford to get the sack of flour, which she carried with her as a proof of the statement that she had gone to the mill. Fortunately she reached her home safely, and apparently the incident after that was forgotten by the other members of the household.

But she was in a state of high nervous tension until she could be assured of the safety of the Continental army. She waited eagerly for the departure of the

British. It was about forty-eight hours after her return from Whitemarsh that the beating of drums and
the marching of many feet announced the departure
of the troops for the purpose of surprising Washington. Lydia Darrah stood on the sidewalk as the glittering cavalcades passed by, apparently a non-impor-
tant unit in the mass of spectators, but actually the he-
roine, if not the most important figure, of the drama
that was to be enacted. After the last of the soldiers
had departed she retired to her room in a fever of apprehension that was not to be allayed until she had
received definite news of the encounter between the
two armies.

General Howe was in high good spirits. He felt
that he was going to catch the " old fox " sleeping, and
the thought made him chuckle with delight. The town
was full of Tories, too, and many of them would not
have been displeased if the " rebels " received a crushing blow. But Lydia Darrah, in her darkened chamber, hoped and prayed that all might go well with
Washington and his men.

In the meantime, at Whitemarsh, preparations for
meeting the enemy were going on in the Continental
army. Washington was impressed with the information brought to him by Lieutenant Colonel Craig. On
the day of the 4th the Commander-in-chief received
word from Captain Allen McLane, a vigilant officer,
which confirmed the warning carried to the camp by
Lydia Darrah. He made his dispositions to receive
the meditated assault, and in the meantime sent Mc-
Lane, with 100 men, to reconnoiter. This gallant offi-

cer met the van of the enemy at eleven o'clock at night on the Germantown road, attacked it and forced it to change its line of march.

But it was three o'clock in the morning before the alarm gun announced the approach of the main body of the British army. They appeared at daybreak and took their position at Chestnut Hill within three miles of Washington's right wing. Here the invaders met with a second surprise. Far from being unprepared, a detachment of the Pennsylvania State Militia sallied forth and gave battle to the redcoats. It was a draw, with a few dead and wounded on each side, and the British general in charge exclaimed:

" They don't seem to be a bit surprised! "

General Howe passed the day in reconnoitering and at night changed his ground and moved to a hill on the left within a mile of the American line. He wanted to get into action, but Washington, with great military shrewdness, declined to accommodate him. There were several sharp skirmishes at Edge Hill, and other points thereabouts, in which Morgan's Riflemen and the Maryland Militia were concerned, but no general engagement.

On the morning of the seventh there was every evidence that Howe meditated an attack on the left wing. This was what Washington most desired and his hopes ran high as he prepared for a warm and decisive action. In the course of the day he rode through every brigade explaining how the attack was to be met and exhorting the men to remember that they were fighting in the cause of liberty. He urged them to depend mainly upon the bayonet and to be on the aggressive always. Both his words and his manner impressed them, but especially his manner, for Washington had a demeanor at once grave and determined, which filled his followers with confidence.

The day wore on to its close with nothing but minor skirmishes. The reports show that Morgan's Riflemen and the Maryland Militia under Colonel Gist did brave work in this regard. An attack was next expected during the night, but it never occurred. The spirit displayed by the Americans, and especially their preparedness, had a discouraging effect upon the invaders.

When the first gray tints of dawn appeared it was seen that the British army was in motion again. But they did not advance toward the Americans. On the contrary they filed off to the right where long strings of fires were lit; behind these fires the redcoats silently departed in the direction of Philadelphia.

They had come on a fool's errand — like the king's soldiers in the couplet, they had marched up the hill and then marched down again.

Washington immediately detached light firing parties to fall upon the rear of the departing army, but they had secured too good a start to be very seriously damaged. The Continentals did, however, succeed in worrying the redcoats and in making them regret they had left Philadelphia.

Washington was sorry that there had not been a battle, and writing to the President of Congress at the time said:

" I sincerely wish they had made an attack; as the issue in all probability, from the disposition of our troops and the strong situation of our camp, must have been fortunate and happy. At the same time I must add, that reason, prudence and every principle of policy forbade us from quitting our post to attack them. Nothing but success would have justified the measure; and this could not have been expected from their position."

It was a sorry procession of Englishmen that filed through the streets of Philadelphia after this historic retreat — because it can only be called a retreat. They had gone out with high hopes; they had returned — figuratively speaking — with their tails between their legs. They had expected to throw themselves upon a camp of sleeping and unprepared men; they had encountered a spirited and fully prepared foe. The Tory ladies who lined the sidewalks of the city felt sorry for the non-conquering heroes. But one woman watched that mournful march with pleasure, the woman who was chiefly responisble for it — Lydia Darrah.

On the night after the return of the British troops the Adjutant-General of the army sent for Lydia Darrah. He requested her to come to his room as he wished to put to her some important questions. She followed, quaking in her shoes. She felt that some one had betrayed her, and prepared to suffer the consequences.

" What I wish to know," he said, after she had been

seated, " is whether any of your family was up after
eight o'clock on the night that I conferred with the
other officers in your sitting-room."

She shook her poke-bonneted head.

" Thee knows that we all went to bed at eight
o'clock," she answered.

" I know that *you* were asleep," he said with em-
phasis, " because I had to knock at your chamber door
three times before you were aroused.   But I wondered
if any one else was about."

" Why? "

" Because some one must have given Washington
information concerning our march.   I know you were
in bed; you say the others were also.   I can't imagine
who gave us away unless the walls had ears.   When
we reached Whitemarsh we found all their cannon
mounted and the soldiers ready to receive us.   Consequently, after wasting days in marching and counter-
marching, we were compelled to come back here like
a pack of fools."

" I sympathize with thee," she said, but if one could
have peeped beneath the folds of that poke bonnet one
would have sworn there was a twinkle in those demure
eyes and a smile of satisfaction upon that placid face.

And who will have the heart to find fault with the
brave Quakeress for the twinkle, the smile and the
white lie?

IX

DOCTOR STEIBER AND THE MYSTERY
OF THE FRANCO-PRUSSIAN WAR

IX

DOCTOR STEIBER AND THE MYSTERY
OF THE FRANCO-PRUSSIAN WAR

ONE of the mysteries that has ever puzzled patriotic Frenchmen is how Germany — in 1870 —
was able to crush France in one of the shortest
and most humiliating wars in history. The bravery,
the unquestioned courage of the French soldier, in
every war prior to and since 1870, has been universally
conceded. The French troops have often held out
against great odds and acknowledged defeat only after
a long and stubborn resistance. Why did the national
defenses in 1870 fall down like so many houses of
cards? Why was France caught in such an utterly
unprepared condition? Why was it that so many
French troops were captured like rats in a trap? In
a word, what was the mystery of the Franco-Prussian
War?

The answer is simple. They were out-spied, and
the man behind the mystery was Doctor Steiber, Chief
of the Prussian Secret Service.

He confessed afterwards, and it has since been cor-
roborated from many reliable sources, that two armies
were responsible for the defeat of France in the
Franco-Prussian War. One was Steiber's army of
spies which invaded the country in 1867, 1868, and

129

1869, and the other was the German military army which came in 1870.

Steiber was a man with untiring push, unlimited persistence and an unpleasant personality. He had big ears, a big nose, shifty eyes and an irritating smile. Like a certain character made famous by Dickens, he was always washing his hands in invisible water. He was cordially disliked by many of the German officers, but was a favorite of Prince Bismarck, and that, of course, turned the scales in his favor. Napoleon's chief spy was an Alsatian smuggler, while Bismarck's secret service agent was a socialist. At least that is what he was before he attracted the attention of the German Prime Minister. After that he believed absolutely in the sacred rights of property.

It was in 1864 that he first performed any work of consequence outside of Germany. About that time Bismarck began to have designs upon Bohemia, but before attacking that country the prudent head of the State Department desired to get all of the inside information that was possible. He looked about him for an instrument, and his gaze fell upon the erstwhile socialist.

In the latter part of 1864 Steiber set out for Bohemia. As the people of that country were very religious he went in the guise of a peddler of religious statutes. He traveled from one town to another gaining the confidence of the honest and simple minded people, and acquiring a vast fund of information concerning the forts and defenses and the general state of military preparedness — or unpreparedness. He remained there for many months and had the assistance of a number of lesser spies. When he returned to Germany he was able to place this data in the hands of Bismarck, who, in turn, gave it to Moltke.

On the strength of this report it was decided to invade Bohemia, and many thousands of well-drilled, well-officered and well-fed troops advanced upon what might fairly be called a helpless country. It was one victory after another until Bohemia was entirely subjugated. Doctor Steiber accompanied the German army in its victorious march, but more in the rôle of an informer than a warrior. Naturally many of the German officers were aware of the character of his work, and some of them were outspoken in their disgust. Many of them refused to eat at the same mess with him. Bismarck was in the field on one occasion and Steiber complained to him of the affronts that had been placed upon him.

" They go out of their way to show their dislike of me," he said.

" Well, what of it?" was the gruff query.

" They should be disciplined," he insisted, "because I am merely carrying out your orders."

" You think so?"

" I do."

" Well," was the shrewd response, "I will teach them a lesson in my own way."

And so he did. And it took the form of having Doctor Steiber dine with him in his own tent.

During the course of the invasion Steiber was made Governor of Braum, the capital of Moravia, thus becoming a sort of glorified chief of police. In this position, as might be expected, there were many rich pickings, a fact that was not overlooked by the thrifty ex-socialist. This was not all. He was decorated, and the medal bestowed upon him was pinned on his ample bosom by Moltke. That soldier, like Bismarck, was eminently practical. As if to justify himself he said on one occasion:

"One must not confine oneself to giving money to spies. One must know how to show them honor when they deserve it."

After the Bohemian business had been concluded, Doctor Steiber had a period of comparative ease. He rested, so to speak, on his "laurels." He prospered in a worldly sense, and was happy in possessing the confidence and the favor of those who were high in Prussian officialdom. He knew the time would come when his peculiar services would be in demand. Meanwhile he continued with the routine work of the Secret Service office. The call for bigger things came sooner than he anticipated. It was early one day in June, 1867, that he received a summons from Bismarck.

He dropped everything and hastened to the home of the Prime Minister. He found him alone, and at breakfast. Bismarck greeted him with lazy, good natured tolerance, and bade him be seated until he had finished, what was to him at that moment the most important thing in the world — his meal. While Steiber waited he had a chance to study the personality of this remarkable man.

It seemed to him that Bismarck was all body. He was impressed more than anything else with the bulkiness of the Prime Minister. He was massive,— "as big as a mountain," as he afterwards expressed it. For the rest of it, there was nothing to dispel the popular conception of the man, the broad shoulders, thick neck, grisly mustache, bushy eyebrows and grim determined look.

"Steiber," said the Prime Minister between bites, "we have real work cut out for you now — work and not mere child's play."

"And might I inquire what it is, your Excellency?" asked the spy respectfully.

"All in good time," was the playful response. "For the present you will see that we have important business on hand."

This allusion to the meal spread before the man of blood and iron, of course, brought the expected laugh from the Chief of the Prussian Secret Service. And he sat and watched with amazement the gastronomic powers of the great man. He had heard of Bismarck's ability in this line, but had never witnessed anything like the present exhibition. He had been told that on one historic occasion, in the presence of the Emperor, the count drained a quart of champagne from a loving cup without pausing for breath, and now he believed it.

The breakfast which was to satisfy the morning appetite of Bismarck was an average meal — the kind that ordinarily pleased him. It consisted of six eggs, a beefsteak, several slices of pheasant, a dish of fried potatoes, a plate of rye bread, cakes, three cups of coffee and a quart of red wine. Two large hunting dogs hovered about the table, and from time to time during the meal the Prime Minister tossed bits of meat to them. After he had concluded his breakfast Bismarck leaned back in his chair with a sigh of satisfaction. Presently he reached for a long-stemmed pipe, and lighting it, sent clouds of smoke about the room. He was at peace with all the world — and with Bismarck, too.

"Now," he said lazily, and yet with a sort of determination, "for business."

Steiber realized, when his patron arose, that Bismarck was a tall man, a fact that was not always apparent because of his great bulk. The Prime Minister laid his pipe aside and paced the floor as he talked. Presently he sat down again and lit a cigar. And during the remainder of the interview he continued smoking. He was what is popularly called a "chain smoker," each cigar being lighted by the stub of its predecessor.

His instructions were clean cut and to the point. Steiber was to go into France and spy out that country for the benefit of Prussia. He was to have unlimited means and all of the assistance he might require. He was to get plans of forts and defenses generally; to ascertain the size and condition of the French army and to learn all that was possible of the secrets of the French War Office. In a word, he was to repeat, in France, what he had already done in Bohemia.

When Bismarck dismissed Steiber the spy had the greatest commission of his career. He had little doubt

PRINCE VON BISMARCK

of his ability to execute it.   He feared no man, except
possibly Bismarck.   The meeting and the parting of
the two men on that eventful day might be called historic.   The Chancellor even went so far as to lay his
hand on the shoulder of his agent.

" Remember the Fatherland! "

The builder of the German Empire stood there with
all of the immensity and impressiveness of a bronze
statue, and as the spy left he carried with him the
remembrance of the tall figure, the broad shoulders,
the thick neck, the grisly mustache, the keen eyes, and
the grim, determined look.   And as a background
there was the table littered with the remains of that
amazing meal and the Japanned plate filled with smoldering cigar stumps.

Steiber went forth proud and boastful and with the
vision of more medals to cover his ample breast.   His
big ears seemed to become bigger, his enormous nose
appeared to grow larger, and his shifty eyes were fairly
dancing with delight.

He hurried to his office and began to prepare for the
campaign of espionage.   It was not the sort of thing
to plan in an hour or a day.   He devoted weeks of
labor to the task.   Maps of all kinds were consulted
and all sorts of secret information was brought from
all sorts of impossible hiding-places.   He considered
next the men that should go with him and the various
branches of work that should be assigned to them, and
finally the job was completed with the thoroughness for
which the official German is noted.

When Steiber started on this secret invasion of

France he took with him two lieutenants, Zernicki and Kalten. Their work lay in the military line. They visited fortifications in all parts of France; they carried cameras with them, and in spite of the regulations forbidding such things, they made photographs of the defenses and even of the cannon in the forts. Disguised as peddlers they made their way into the various garrisons and studied the methods of the drill, discovered the number of men attached to each of the regiments, and altogether obtained a mass of information that could not possibly have been gleaned from blue books or official publications.

In the same manner men were sent to the different navy yards. They explored the warships and cruisers and obtained data which was promptly forwarded to the Foreign Office in Berlin. Napoleon III reigned over France at this time, and while he must have known the danger that threatened his country by reason of German aggression, he apparently made no effort to avert it. Spies ran about almost under his nose and he could not see them. Some years before this, when it was reported that the people of Paris were discontented, he said:

"Well, gild the dome of Les Invalides — that will give them something to look at."

And, indeed, he gave the people a great deal to distract them from the fear of both poverty and war. He was largely responsible for making Paris the most beautiful city in the world. He laid out the magnificent boulevards, built the great sewers and in other ways made the city the joy and pride of the inhabitants.

There had long been ill feeling smoldering between France and Germany and the two countries were on the verge of war in 1866. But this significant fact was lost on Napoleon III, and the German spies, when they came into France, found a fertile soil to cultivate.

Steiber did not stop at learning the secrets of the army and navy. His spies even went to Versailles and were to be found in public and semi-public institutions everywhere. They consisted of both men and women. If one went into a restaurant the waiter who attended to his wants was likely to be a German spy. If a Frenchwoman — possibly the wife of an army or naval officer — went to her dressmaker's she was fitted by a female who probably was on the payroll of Doctor Steiber. At one time, it is hinted, there were five thousand Prussian spies working on French territory. Never was a country so overrun by the secret agents of a foreign power.

Finally, in the latter part of 1869, Steiber completed his work and started back to Berlin. And all this time the complacent French Emperor and the credulous French people, were in ignorance of how they had been betrayed by the thousands of foreign visitors. Steiber, Zernicki and Kalten carried several large trunks with them — trunks that were zealously guarded by day and by night. These trunks contained plans of all sorts and reports that had been returned by the myriads of spies under the Chief of the Prussian Secret Service. Suppose these trunks had been captured and confiscated by the French police? Suppos Steiber and his emissaries had been arrested while

they were still on French territory?   Is it too much to
say that it would have changed the course of history?

Steiber on his return to Berlin went direct to the
home of the Chancellor.   He found him, as before,
resting after one of those meals for which he was
famous.   It seemed very familiar, the broad shoulders,
thick neck, grisly mustache, bushy eyebrows and grim,
determined look.   He greeted his agent with a playful
manner and bade him tell all he knew.   That consumed
some time, for it must be remembered that Steiber and
his corps of assistants had spent more than two years
in France.   It is true that much of the information had
been sent as fast as it was collected, but Bismarck
wanted direct, first-hand news from his trusted servant.

And while he talked the Chancellor smoked one cigar
after another and occasionally tossed bits of meat to
the dogs that were constantly by his side.   After the
interview Steiber received another medal to add to the
collection he had already acquired.   And then Berlin,
so to speak, having set the stage, calmly awaited the
course of events.

The climax came quicker than was anticipated.
Napoleon demanded that the King of Prussia should
bind himself by an autograph letter never to support
Prince Leopold as a candidate for the Spanish crown.
Bismarck, confident in his power, and fortified by the
knowledge that he had of the French unpreparedness,
calmly refused to lay the request before the monarch.

This was an intolerable slight from one who was
regarded as a subordinate.   A few days after this the

French Ambassador chanced to meet the King in a public walk at Ems, and there and then asked him to give the desired promise. King William refused, with indignation, to transact business under such circumstances and later notified the Ambassador that he would not be given an audience at the royal palace.

Napoleon regarded this as the insult direct, and as a consequence of the incident war was declared between the two countries. The people, of course, were unfamiliar with real conditions. They did not know that their country had been infested with foreign spies and that they were utterly unprepared for war. They were angered at the apparent slight that had been put upon the French nation and they were filled with a burning patriotism. In no time the streets of Paris were filled with but one cry:

" On to Berlin ! "

Napoleon, heading a hastily mobilized army, marched north and camped at Metz, whence he proposed crossing the Rhine into Germany. But the Germans, instead of waiting for this, invaded France, hurrying directly toward Paris. The scorn and indignation of the people was intense. Marshal McMahon fought bravely, but was driven back, and Marshal Bazaine, after a struggle, was driven within the fortifications at Metz. Everything had come about as the Germans anticipated. A large part of the French army was shut up in a trap, while the remainder struggled for existence.

On the eve of the first of September, 1870, the King of Prussia arrived at Versailles and took up his lodgings in the palace belonging to the Duc de Persigny. And with him was Doctor Steiber, gloating and continually washing his hands in invisible water. Was not all of this his work? Had he not spied out the land? Had he not invaded France before the army arrived? In a word, was not this conquest of the army but a confirmation of his victory of espionage? He was more boastful than ever and his big ears and big nose were everywhere in evidence.

While the King of Prussia ruled like a conqueror, Steiber played the tyrant in his own way. He had large powers and he did not hesitate to use them. . One incident will show the character of the man. A wealthy and popular young Frenchman, Monsieur de Raynal, had returned to Versailles from his honeymoon, arriving just in time to meet the German invaders. He kept a diary of the happenings of the invasion. It was not much — merely a colorful account, day by day, of the doings of the invaders. Perhaps he did not draw a flattering picture of the Prussians. How could he? The confiscation of the offending document and maybe the temporary imprisonment of the writer would have been ample punishment, if indeed, any were necessary. But the beggar on horseback did not think so.

He decreed that the gallant Frenchman should be executed. Friends of the gentleman interceded and asked clemency on the ground that he was but newly married and on his honeymoon. Steiber spread out his big hands, shrugged his ugly shoulders and said, " Ah, but that only makes my task the more painful."

Even the German soldiers entered their protest. But
in spite of it Monsieur de Raynal was executed. And
Steiber rubbed his hands, washing them, as ever, in
invisible water. But all the water in creation would
not wash the blood of innocent victims from those dirty
hands!

While this was going on in Versailles the brave Mc-
Mahon was pressing forward to the relief of Bazaine.
Presently he reached Sedan, where a great battle was
fought, resulting in the decisive defeat of the French.
On the evening of the following day Napoleon — Napoleon the Little — as he was derisively called by Vic-
tor Hugo — sent a letter to the King of Prussia in
which he said:

" Not being able to die at the head of my troops, I
can only resign my sword into the hands of Your
Majesty."

Following this, Napoleon, with McMahon and 80,-
000 prisoners of war, surrendered to the enemy.
Three days later. the Emperor was deposed and France
made a Republic. So rapidly did one event follow
another. Bazaine held out until October when he,
with 6,000 officers and 170,000 men, laid down their
arms. Bazaine was afterwards tried and sentenced to
degradation and death for having failed in his duty to
France. The sentence was commuted to twenty years'
imprisonment, from which he effected his escape.

Then came the Third Republic, the siege of Paris
and the treaty of peace in February, 1871; France
agreed to give up all of German-speaking Lorraine and
the whole of Alsace and to pay 5,000,000,000 francs to

Germany.   The story of how the inhabitants of Alsace were compelled to choose between becoming German citizens or leaving the province is a sad one.   The melancholy procession, when fifty thousand of them left their homes and their all and marched into France on the 30th of September, 1872, will never be forgotten.

The great statue in the Place de la Concorde in Paris, with one of its marble figures draped in mourning on national holidays, has been a constant reminder to posterity.

When the victorious Germans returned to Berlin Doctor Steiber was with them — proud and boastful as ever.   The order of the Red Eagle was added to his numerous decorations, and it was reputed that he became a millionaire in addition.

The Franco-Prussian War — or at least the result of that war — has ever been a mystery to patriotic Frenchmen.   But the solution of it may be found in that secret invasion of spies led by Steiber and his unscrupulous lieutenants.

X

THE ADVENTURE OF PRIVATE MORGAN
IN THE CAMP OF CORNWALLIS

X

THE ADVENTURE OF PRIVATE MORGAN
IN THE CAMP OF CORNWALLIS

THIS is the story of how a private soldier in the New Jersey Brigade displayed remarkable shrewdness and unusual courage, and participated in the glory of one of the most successful campaigns of the Revolutionary War by acting as the agent of General Lafayette in entering the British lines, and obtaining valuable information concerning the movements of Cornwallis.

It is quite possible that other private soldiers of the Continental army may have performed exploits just as thrilling in their nature, but Charles Morgan had the good fortune to be the man of the hour, and the fact that he secured precisely the information that was desired at one of the critical stages of the Revolution stamps him as a man of more than ordinary intelligence and resourcefulness. Nothing succeeds like success, and Morgan succeeded far beyond his most sanguine expectations.

General Lafayette had reached a point in his campaign where he desired to obtain accurate information regarding the resources and intentions of the enemy. He had been worrying Cornwallis for several weeks and in the summer of 1781 the British commander reached Virginia after vainly pursuing the French general and destroying millions of dollars' worth of property. Eventually he reached Yorktown, on a narrow peninsula at the mouth of the York River. He had no desire to go to this place, but did so because there was nothing else to do under the circumstances. During his chase of Lafayette he boastingly said: "The boy cannot escape me," but to his amazement the youngster with a larger army had turned around and begun to chase him. It was then that Cornwallis had retreated to Yorktown in order to get help by sea from New York. There he began the work of fortifying himself, little dreaming that he was placing himself in a trap from which it would be almost impossible to escape. While he was waiting for the soldiers to arrive from New York a French fleet of warships under Count de Grasse was coming to block him. This was the great opportunity of the Continental army to strike a blow that might be heard around the world. Washington's plan, and it was concurred in by Lafayette, was to march rapidly south from the Hudson to Yorktown, and, with the help of the French fleet on one side and Lafayette and his army on the other, to capture Cornwallis with his whole force. Needless to say, a movement of this character required an immense sum of money for provisions, pay and powder. In this crisis Robert Morris, patriot and Philadelphia financier, came to the rescue and furnished nearly $1,500,000 for the work of putting the patriot army in the proper condition.

Lafayette disposed his forces with great military

ability, but there were some points in the proposed plan
of campaign which were not quite clear to his mind.
He was anxious to procure exact information of the
strength of the forces under Cornwallis, and if possible
to learn the exact nature of that general's plan of campaign.   He looked about him for some courageous and
intelligent man who could obtain the information he
desired.   His choice fell upon Charles Morgan, a member of the New Jersey Brigade, who had attracted his
attention by bravery in battle.   He sent for Morgan
and told him that he considered him a proper agent for
the accomplishment of his purpose and proposed that
he should enter the British camp in the character of a
deserter, but in reality a spy.

The soldier was delighted at the thought of being
selected for such a hazardous enterprise.   Lafayette
at that time was in all the glory of his young manhood.
To Morgan he was the very embodiment of romance.
He had looked upon him for months with wonder and
delight.   He was to him the bright particular hero of
the Revolution. 'That a man should give up family,
friends and fortune, and all of the prospects of a great
career, should leave his own country to go to a foreign
shore for the purpose of casting his lot with the struggling colonists, made him sublimely heroic. The
courtly airs of the young nobleman also captivated the
imagination of the New Jersey soldier.   Morgan,
before entering the army, had been a farmer.   He was
sturdy and wholesome, yet without the benefits of an
education, and the French general dazzled him with his
simplicity of manner no less than by his natural

assumption of authority. He could scarcely believe
his ears when he was told that he was to act as the
confidential agent of the General in such an important
enterprise.

"This mission," said Lafayette, 'is a dangerous
one. It may cost you your life. Under the circumstances I am not willing to order you to do what I
desire. If you go to the camp of Cornwallis it must
be a voluntary act, and with the full understanding of
its possible consequences."

"I am perfectly willing," was the prompt reply,
" and am glad to serve you and my country."

The Marquis beamed upon him with satisfaction in
his countenance. He spoke to him in a fatherly manner and added:

"Now, if there is any assistance you require from
me, either with money or men, do not hesitate to ask
for it."

Morgan shook his head.

"None at all. I am glad to take the risk, but I
would not like to do this work unless my motives are
perfectly understood. I only ask one thing and that
is that if I should be detected and executed you will
cause a notice to be inserted in the New Jersey papers
saying that I was acting under the orders of my commanding officer."

The required condition was readily accepted by the
General, who then proceeded to explain just what he
wished to ascertain.

That night Morgan entered the British lines in the
guise of a deserter, and was warmly welcomed by the

GENERAL LAFAYETTE

English soldiers. The officer who first met him looked at Morgan with some curiosity, and said:

"Why did you leave the rebels? Were you afraid that they were about to be defeated?"

Morgan protested warmly that he had no such thought in his mind.

"I have been with the American army from the beginning of the war," he said, "and I went into the contest with all my heart and soul. While I served with General Washington I was perfectly satisfied and I would have gone until the end, but when they put me under the charge of a Frenchman I felt that it was time to call a halt. I was unwilling to fight under a foreigner. I did not like it, I chafed under it, and finally I made up my mind to desert, and here I am."

With this story, which was given with an air of the greatest plausibility, the British were satisfied. They received the supposed deserter without suspicion and assigned him to duty as a soldier in one of the English regiments. But before going on actual duty the young man was taken to Cornwallis and his story repeated. The British general was attired in all the glory of his high office and the members of his staff presented a glittering array of gold lace. Morgan could not help but contrast their prosperous appearance with the shabby and threadbare condition of the American army. Cornwallis was an imposing looking man who evidently was filled with the importance of his rank. He spoke harshly enough to his officers, but assumed a kindly manner with the deserter from the American ranks.

"How many men has Lafayette under his command?" he asked.

Morgan gave a quick reply, giving the number at much less than the actual force under the French general.

"How long will it take the Marquis to cross the James River?" asked Cornwallis.

"Three hours, my lord," was the answer.

"Three hours," exclaimed Cornwallis. "Don't you think it is more likely to take three days?"

"Not at all, my lord," was the response. "The Marquis has a certain number of boats, and each boat will carry a certain number of men, and if your Lordship will take the trouble of calculating you can find that he can cross the stream in about three hours."

Cornwallis turned to his officers and began speaking in an undertone to them. There was much discussion and a great deal of shaking of heads, and finally the Earl said in the hearing of Morgan:

"The scheme will not do. We will have to change some of the lines."

After that Morgan was assigned to his position with one of the English regiments. He was a hale fellow well met, and it did not take him long to win their confidence. The circumstances under which he had come to the British army gave him considerable latitude and he was able to go and come pretty much as he pleased. He talked freely with the officers and they, in turn, regarding him as a zealous convert to their cause, did not hesitate to furnish him with the kind of information which he most desired. Once or twice after that he was called before Cornwallis and cross-questioned concerning the plans of the American army. He stood this ordeal with amazing self-possession, and by his native shrewdness managed to obtain much more information than he gave, the difference being that his news was the product of his imagination, while the information he obtained was accurate and clearly outlined the movement of the forces under Cornwallis.

Morgan became the special friend of four of the men in his regiment. After some weeks they began to tell him of their troubles. They looked upon him as a superior and indicated by their manner a desire to follow his advice. Each soldier was allowed a certain amount of grog each day, and he further increased their regard for him by dividing his liquor with them. Presently they began to complain of the privations to which they had been subjected in the British camp. He listened with ready sympathy and when he felt that the time was ripe assured them privately that the American army was at the present time enjoying a plentiful supply of provisions. He also assured them that the victory of the American cause was as certain as that the sun would rise in the morning. Finally, he proposed that they should all desert and go over to the American army. The Englishmen were familiar with the passwords and numbered the sentries among their personal friends. This helped to make Morgan's return to his own army comparatively easy.

Their plans were carefully made and shortly before midnight the five men, headed by Morgan, left the British camp. They were halted by a sentinel, who told them that they would not be permitted to leave the British lines without a passport.

"We are only on a lark," Morgan assured him, "and if you will let us go by we will promise to return before daylight."

"But if I do, it will get me into trouble," insisted the man.

"Not at all," was the ready retort. "You let us go and we will see that no harm comes to you."

As a further proof of friendship the American produced the canteen which he had brought with him and gave the sentinel a liberal draught of the rum. They remained talking with him for a few minutes and then treated him to a second drink. After that he was in the humor to pass the entire regiment without either explanations or passports.

The experience which they had with this first man was repeated with two other sentinels, and eventually they found themselves outside of the British lines and headed toward the American camp.

It was an unpleasant journey. They had to make their way through swampy ground and several times found themselves up to their ankles in mud and water. The British deserters were very much depressed and at one stage of the trip would have gladly returned to their own camp, but Morgan had gone too far to permit anything of that kind. He continued to furnish them with liquor and in this way kept their courage buoyed up to the sticking point. Finally, just before daylight, they found themselves within sight of the American lines. The sun was shining when Morgan

reached the American camp with the four British
deserters trailing at his heels. He was received with
great delight by his fellow patriots and almost immediately escorted to the headquarters of General Lafayette. The Marquis hastened to meet him and eagerly
clapped him on the back.

"My friend," he said, "I am delighted to see you
again — to see you in the flesh."

"I have carried out your instructions," said Morgan,
modestly.

"So I presume. But who is it you have with you?"

"These are four British soldiers who have decided
to give themselves to the cause of liberty."

The General directed that the recruits be fed and
clothed and enlisted in the regiment to which Morgan
was attached. After that he made Morgan sit down
and tell the story of his stay in the camp of Cornwallis. This he was able to do with intelligence and in
great detail. Lafayette thus obtained the information
which he desired. He praised his messenger highly
and told him that he would commend him to the good
offices of General Washington. In the meantime he
proposed to promote him to the rank of corporal, with
the promise of still further promotion in the near
future. But the volunteer spy shook his head.

"I thank you for your goodness. I appreciate it
greatly, but I do not desire to go above the rank of an
ordinary private. I have ability for a common soldier,
but should I be promoted, my ability may not be equal
to the occasion, and I would thus lose my character."

General Lafayette laughed heartily at this unusual

display of modesty, but assured Morgan that his services would not be forgotten and that at the proper time
he would be rewarded for his sacrifice and his heroism.

Lafayette was now in a position to act with intelligence.   The information that had been brought to him
by his spy fortunately did not make it necessary for him
to change his plan of campaign.   He was in communication with other Continental officers and kept constantly informed of the progress of the campaign.   He
discovered many other things; that Clinton, at the head
of the British forces in New York, was under the
impression that Washington was getting ready to
attack him.   Washington encouraged him to think so.
In order that the British general should not be disillu-
sioned, the American continued to make every possible
preparation for moving against New York.   So cleverly was this ruse carried on that the members of
Washington's own army supposed that he was really
getting ready to attack Clinton.   When at length
everything was just as he wished it, Washington suddenly broke camp and conducted his entire force with
all possible speed across the country to the head of
Chesapeake Bay and thus by vessels to Yorktown.   It
was truly a critical time in the Revolutionary War.
While Washington was continuing his southern movement Lafayette and his army closed in on the other
side.   The British realized that they were gradually
becoming the victims of a vast enveloping movement.
Cornwallis put his spy glass to his eye and peered over
the walls of his fortified town.   On one side he beheld
the French fleet, on the other side Washington's troops,

and on still another, Lafayette's army. The Americans, 16,000 strong, were gradually but surely coming closer and closer. Cornwallis held out with great bravery for three weeks, but the constant rain of shells and hot shot made his position almost impossible. Finally, seeing that it was useless to struggle against fate, he surrendered. His army marched out on the 19th of October, 1781, to the tune of "The World's Upside Down," and it was — at least to the British. They were dazed and could not understand how such a powerful army and such a great empire should fall victims to what seemed to be a handful of untrained farmers. But in spite of their feeling it was over, and they were the vanquished.

The fall of Yorktown practically ended the war of the Revolution. Washington had conquered. Lafayette's confidence in the struggling colonists was fully vindicated and his great respect for George Washington increased. As has been said, it was the victory of a great and good man in a great and good cause.

The news of the surrender was sent post-haste to London. The excited messenger who announced the sad tidings to Lord North, the Prime Minister of the British Government, afterwards said that that functionary threw up his arms as though he had received a shot and cried dramatically:

"It is all over!"

And so it was; and in the victory at Yorktown none of the Continental troops fought more bravely or showed to greater advantage than those who served under the leadership of Lafayette. Among the privates in the New Jersey Brigade none fought with greater courage than Charles Morgan, who had served as the personal spy of the great Frenchman in the camp of Cornwallis.   But in his case virtue and courage had to be their own reward.   Many of the soldiers who deserved great honor were compelled to go unrewarded, and Charles Morgan was apparently one of these, for after his exploit, and the ending of the war, his name does not appear in any of the records of that great event.   Like many other deserving men, he was lost in the mists of obscurity.

XI

THE MYSTERIOUS AND ROMANTIC CASE
OF GENERAL NAPPER TANDY

XI

THE MYSTERIOUS AND ROMANTIC CASE OF GENERAL NAPPER TANDY

DURING the Napoleonic wars scores of military spies were sent from England and France, and most of them performed their work so well that posterity has not even been given the benefit of their names. Perhaps the most industrious of these was a man who was simply known as " O." He was constantly in communication with the English Government and he kept Pitt, the English Prime Minister, informed of the movements of certain Irishmen who had left their own country to enlist under the banner of Napoleon.

One of the most conspicuous of these was General Napper Tandy, who urged upon the Man of Destiny the advisability of attacking England by making a descent upon the coast of Ireland. For more than a half-century the greatest mystery hovered about the name and the identity of General Napper Tandy. But it was finally cleared up through the persistence and the painstaking efforts of William J. Fitzpatrick, the Irish historian, but only after he had secured the permission of the English Government to make an examination of the secret archives of Dublin Castle.

As a result of that, we now know that Tandy was an adventurous soul who was willing to fight at the drop of a hat.   He is described in Government reports as an " arch rebel," and it is certain that he took part in various Irish uprisings against the English Government.   He went over to France about 1796 and identified himself with Napoleon.   He was a brave man, with much knowledge of military strategy and undoubtedly made an impression upon one who was regarded as the greatest military strategist of his day.

That Napoleon thought well of the proposed invasion of Ireland is proven by his negotiations with Thomas Addis Emmet.   The correspondence of the great Corsican makes that fact clear.   But Emmet accused him of coldness and indecision on the Irish program, because, instead of going to Ireland in 1798, he changed his plans and went to Egypt.

However, there was never any doubt about the plans of General Tandy, and the manner in which he carried them out is part of the secret history of the times.   A meeting to arrange the details was held in Paris, and was attended by Messrs. Blackwell, Morres, Tandy and Corbett.   Unfortunately for them, there was another person present, and that was the English spy who became known later from the fact that he signed all of his communications to the English Government with the letter " O."

Mr. Fitzpatrick, after the most exhaustive researches, is convinced that this spy was a man named Orr, who had been on Pitt's payroll for a long time.

He had been a thorn in the side of Napoleon for years,
and even before the meeting which Tandy held in Paris
had sent a note to his chief in which he said:

"The grand object of the French is, as they term it
themselves, London. *Delanda Carthago* is their particular end; once in England, they think they would
speedily indemnify themselves for all their expenses
and recruit their ruined finances."

It is certain that "O" was not only present at the
meeting to arrange for the expedition into Ireland, but
that he made suggestions regarding the details of that
historic trip. It is interesting to know that before the
ship set sail full particulars of it had been sent by "O"
to his English employers. He even goes so far as to
make sport of the finances of the French nation at that
time.

"Three generals are to go out on the little expedition," he writes, "and all the money they can muster
between them is thirty louis d'or. One of them, to my
certain knowledge, has but five guineas in all."

Tandy sailed from Dunkirk in the French ship *Anacreon,* which was well stocked with a store of ord-
nance, ammunition, saddles and accouterments. He
was accompanied by a large staff including Corbett
and Blackwell. One of his aides-de-camp was Orr, the
spy, who kept at his elbow constantly, and learned all of
his most secret plans and hopes. Before the gallant
ship raised anchor there was a conference in the cabin
concerning the most desirable landing place. Maps of
Ireland were consulted, and it was finally decided that
the safest, if not the most secluded stretch of country,

was along the coast of Donegal. General Napper
Tandy was in fine fettle. He wore a most gorgeous
uniform with gold lace and brass buttons, and altogether made an impressive appearance. Like many
brave men, he was a dandy in dress and manner, and
when not fighting, devoted much time to his toilet.
The journey to Ireland was comparatively uneventful,
but all of those aboard the *Anacreon* were glad to see
the shores of the Green Isle.

Tandy was very much concerned regarding another
expedition which had set sail for Ireland about a week
before the departure of his own party. This was in
charge of General Humbert, and was expected to
clear the way for the Tandy invasion. As the ship
approached the shore General Tandy hoisted a green
flag at the masthead of the *Anacreon*. It had on it
the words, " Erin go Bragh," and was intended as a
signal to the Irishmen who were to join in an attack
on the British. He also had with him for distribution,
printed copies of a proclamation addressed to the people of Ireland. It was headed " Liberty or Death,"
and contained a drawing of the Irish harp and the cap
of liberty, and began with the words: " Horrid crimes
have been perpetrated in your country, your friends
have fallen a sacrifice to their devotion to your cause,
and their shadows are around you and call for vengeance." Little did Tandy imagine that copies of these
proclamations were already in the hands of the British,
and that the spy who had forwarded them was then on
the ship with him. If Orr felt any apprehension he did
not show it in his manner, yet he must have known that

if discovered he would have been hanged to the mast arm of the vessel.

Tandy landed in company with General Ray, a French soldier who had seen service with Napoleon. In a short time they were surrounded by a large number of people who looked upon the invaders with amazement and alarm. To them General Ray made a grandiloquent speech, in the course of which he said:

"The soldiers of the Great Nation have landed on your coast well supplied with arms and ammunition of all kinds, and with artillery worked by those who have spread terror amongst the ranks of the best troops in Europe, headed by French officers; they come to break your fetters and restore you to the blessings of liberty. General Napper Tandy is at their head; he has sworn to lead them on to victory or die. Brave Irishmen! The friends of liberty have left their native soil to assist you in reconquering your rights; they will brave the dangers, and glory at the sublime idea of cementing your happiness with their blood."

General Tandy made his headquarters with Mr. Foster, who lived near the coast of Donegal, and after partaking of refreshments he said to that gentleman:

"What news have you got to give me regarding the expedition that landed last week?"

"Not very good — for you at least," said Foster, who was an ardent Royalist. "Part of the French troops landed at Killala, and after winning the battle of Castlebar have been finally compelled to capitulate to Lord Cornwallis."

"I cannot believe it," explained Tandy.

"It is true," was the grim reply, "whether you believe it or not."

In order to assure himself of the truthfulness of the intelligence, General Tandy took forcible possession of the Rutland postoffice, which was kept by Mr. Foster's sister. He opened the newspapers, and to his dismay found that all he had been told was perfectly correct. He realized that the usefulness of his own expedition was destroyed. Indeed, he learned further that a large body of British troops was already on its way to Rutland to capture the latest invaders. Under the circumstances the only thing left for him to do was to retire with as little loss as possible.

The thoughtfulness of this soldier of fortune was illustrated by the fact that he wrote an official letter, signed and sealed, exonerating Foster from blame for not having dispatched his mail bags. He testified that, being in temporary want of accommodation, he was obliged to put Citizen Foster under requisition, and to place sentinels around the island.

It is also a curious fact that he and his officers paid for everything they took, including two pigs and a cow. General Ray, when leaving, removed a gold ring from his finger and presented it to Mrs. Foster as a token of fraternity. Finally, this arch rebel, after paying all of his obligations, discharged a cannon as a farewell note to the people of Donegal.

The *Anacreon* had scarcely started on her way when Foster dispatched two messengers to the proper authorities in the hope that part of the British fleet might intercept the invaders. This was not so easy as

it looked, because Tandy had already told Foster that
they had met several English cruisers on their way to
Ireland and had outsailed them all. The *Anacreon*
proved to be equally successful on its return voyage,
capturing two English ships near the Orkneys after a
stiff engagement, and finally landing Tandy and his
associates in Norway. They landed at Bergen, and
after suffering many trials and tribulations, sought to
reach France by land. The cold became so intense that
people were found frozen to death at the gate of Hamburg. Weary and footsore, Tandy arrived there at
twilight on November 22, 1798.

There he was met by a man named Turner who was
really a spy associated with Orr, but seeming to recog-
nize in him a fellow Irishman, Tandy at once gave him
his confidence and eagerly accepted an invitation from
him to take supper. It has been said, but with how
much truth cannot be vouched for, that Turner was one
of those who was compelled to fly from his native land
on account of the " Wearing of the Green." At all
events there was a verse in the popular ballad which
ran thus :

" I met with Napper Tandy and he took me by the
        hand,
    And he said, ' How's poor old Ireland, and how
        does she stand,
' 'Tis a most distressful country for it's plainly to
        be seen,
    They are hanging men and women for the " Wear-
        ing of the Green." ' "

Little did Tandy suspect that when he accepted this invitation to supper he was walking into a trap that had been set for him. Tandy and his fellow officers were lodged at an inn in Hamburg called the American Arms, and after finishing their meal they retired to their respective rooms. Tandy occupied himself in writing letters. He had many reports to make and explanations concerning the failure of his expedition. He stayed up nearly all night, and about five o'clock in the morning was startled by a loud tapping at his bedroom door. He opened it and an officer walked in followed by Sir James Crawford, British Minister at Hamburg. The officer turned to the Irishman and said:

"I would like to have a look at your passport."

Tandy, although taken by surprise, was perfectly composed.

"If you will wait a moment," he said, "I will get it for you."

Turning around and going over to his trunk he lifted the lid very carefully and took out a pistol which he pointed at the soldier, exclaiming as he did so:

"This is my passport!"

The officer, who had the courage of his convictions, made a rush at him and succeeded in deflecting the aim of the pistol. The next moment the guards rushed in and secured Tandy. Before daylight he and his associates were handcuffed and confined in the local prison by order of Sir James Crawford.

A few hours after the arrest of the culprits Monsieur Maragan, the French resident, wrote to the Senate at Hamburg claiming Tandy and his colleagues as French citizens and threatening to leave the place unless they were released. The British minister opposed this demand very forcibly, and, needless to say, carried his point. The French chargé d'affaires noticed that Tandy was in very poor health and it is said that he offered a large sum to the officer of the guard to permit the Irishman's escape. But the influence of the British minister was strong enough to overcome all obstacles from the French side of the house. The action of the Senate at Hamburg in giving Tandy and his colleagues over to the British created quite a sensation, and was the cause of a prolonged controversy.

That Tandy suffered dreadfully from his confinement is proven by many letters and papers that have since come to light. His sufferings in prison he said were so severe that life was a burden, and more than once he prayed to be led out on the ramparts and shot. John Philpot Curran, writing of his sufferings, says:

" He was confined in a dungeon little larger than a grave. He was loaded with irons; he was chained by an iron that communicated from his árm to his leg and that was so short as to grind into his flesh. Food was cut into shapeless lumps and flung to him by his keepers as he lay on the ground, as if he had been a beast; he had no bed to lie on, not even straw to coil himself up on, if he could have slept."

Corbett, who was one of the prisoners, gives details of the detention which are hardly less painful.

" What happened to me," he writes, " would have naturally discouraged and prevented me from making any new attempts; nevertheless, I managed to correspond with my two companions in misfortune; and we all three stood so well with our guards, the greater number of whom we had gained, that we resolved to arm ourselves and place ourselves at their head to deliver Tandy, who was in another prison, and afterwards to repair to the house of the French ambassador. Our measures were so well taken that we hoped this time at least to recover our liberty in spite of the impediments which fortune might place in our way. But the same traitor who had formerly deranged my plan discovered all to the English minister Crawford, who immediately gave orders that our guard should be changed and even that those of the different posts of Hamburg should be doubled, which continued even to our departure. Such was the result of the last struggle we made to obtain our liberty at Hamburg."

Finally at midnight on September 29, 1799, after ten months' detention, Tandy and his companions were taken from prison and put on an English frigate. As they were leaving, Tandy said to the officer in charge:

" What right did you have to arrest us? You are surely not ignorant of the fact that we were French officers."

The man in charge shrugged his shoulders.

" I merely fulfilled the orders of the minister from England."

By this time France was venting its wrath unreservedly. It denounced the conduct of Hamburg to all states, allied and neutral. It compelled all French consular officers to quit the offending territory and demanded that every agent of Hamburg residing in France should leave in twenty-four hours. The Senate of Hamburg now expressed regret at the occurrence and wrote in this vein to the French authorities.

" Your letter, gentlemen," replied Napoleon, " does not justify you. You have violated the laws of hospitality, a thing which never happened among the most savage hordes of the desert."

A deputation from the Senate of Hamburg arrived at the Tuileries to make a public apology to Napoleon. Once again he expressed his indignation, and when the envoys pleaded national weakness, he exclaimed:

" Well, and had you not the resources of weak states; was it not in your power to let them escape? "

As a result of the incident Napoleon laid a fine of 4,500,000 francs on Hamburg. The payment of this large sum appeased the wrath of the Man of Destiny and also, it is slyly hinted by his secretary, helped to pay Josephine's debts.

In the meanwhile Tandy and his companions had arrived in England. A military escort accompanied them to Rochester and thence over Blackfriars Bridge up Ludgate Hill to Newgate. One of the English newspapers of that time thus describes the event:

" Had Bonaparte and his staff been sent here by Sir Sydney Smith, they could not have excited more curiosity than Tandy and his companions. A vast concourse of people gathered at the landing place and followed the prisoners and their escort to the garrison gates where a new guard was assembled; and so from stage to stage to the end of the journey everybody, old and young, male and female, was anxious to get a peep at this wonderful man now become, from the hope and perverseness of Ministers, a new bone of contention among the Powers of Europe.

"Napper Tandy is a large, big-boned, muscular man, much broken and emaciated.   His hair is quite white from age, cut close behind into his neck, and he appears much enervated.   This is indeed very natural if it be considered that he is nearly seventy years of age and has just suffered a long and rigorous confinement, his mind a constant prey of the most painful suspense.   He wore a large friar's hat, a long silk black greatcoat and military boots, which had a very '*outre*' effect.

"Of Blackwell and Morres, the latter seemed to be five and thirty.   They are two tall, handsome looking men.   They wore military dress and had a very soldier like appearance.   The first named is a man of very enterprising genius, about the middle size and apparently not more than four or five and twenty, and has the look of a foreigner."

Eventually Tandy and his companions were removed to Ireland and were placed at the bar of the King's Bench, when the Attorney General prayed that sentence of death should be passed upon them.   The case was argued for several days and finally Lord Kilwarden ruled that Tandy should be discharged. But he was scarcely given his liberty when he was again arrested in the district where, two years before, he had made a hostile descent from France.   He lay in the jail there for seven months, during which time

GENERAL NAPPER TANDY

great efforts were made to insure the conviction of
what was regarded as a very dangerous character.

Tandy, finding the evidence against him overwhelming, admitted the truth of the indictment and was sentenced to die on the 4th of the following May.   Meanwhile Napoleon, on his return from Egypt, claimed
Tandy as a French general and held an English prisoner of equal rank a hostage for his safety.   At this
stage of the historic affair it was not quite so clear
that the English had a legal claim to the life of a man
who wore the uniform of a French general and who
had been arrested under such peculiar circumstances.
A pardon was eventually made out for him on condition of banishment to Botany Bay.   He indignantly
refused it, but was finally induced to accept it on the
ground that all that was required was merely the name
of transportation, and that if he pleased, it might appear to the world as if he had made his escape at sea.

Napper Tandy arrived at Bordeaux on the 14th of
March, 1802, where he was received with military honors.   Bordeaux was illuminated and the old rebel was
promoted to the rank of a general of division.   In the
midst of his vindication, as he termed it, he read with
real horror a speech of Pelham's in Parliament saying
that he owed his life to the useful information and
discoveries he had given to the British Government.
Instantly he addressed a letter to Pelham branding the
statement as audacious and false.   Mr. Elliott repeated
in Parliament the taunt cast by Pelham, and spoke of
Tandy's ignorance and insignificant birth.   Tandy immediately challenged him to a duel, saying: " A

French officer must not be insulted with impunity, and
you, as well as the country which gave me birth and
that which has adopted me, shall find that I will preserve the honor of my station."

When eight weeks had elapsed and Elliott had failed
to reply, Tandy at once proclaimed him " A calumni-
ator, liar and poltroon."

The most curious part of the whole business is that
General Tandy never knew that he had been betrayed
by a spy who was serving under him as an aide-de-
camp.   His private character was as clean as a hound's
tooth, a fact that led one of his friends to say that
" it furnished no ground to doubt the integrity of his
public one."

But his experiences in and out of prison undermined
his health, and after a lingering illness, he died at
Bordeaux in 1803.   By one of the curious decrees of
destiny George Orr, the spy, lived and prospered long
after Tandy's death, and, if rumor be correct, managed to accumulate not only English but French gold!

XII

HOW MONSIEUR DE MEINAU HELPED TO
MAKE JEROME BONAPARTE KING OF
WESTPHALIA

HOW MONSIEUR DE MEINAU HELPED TO MAKE JEROME BONAPARTE KING OF WESTPHALIA

A MONG all of the world's famous impostors it is doubtful if any could hold a candle to Monsieur de Meinau. Monsieur did not always have such a dignified name. Originally, it will be recalled, he was an Alsatian smuggler and had the plain every-day appellation of Schulmeister. But as Napoleon's chief spy his rise to fame and fortune was both sure and sudden. He was lavishly rewarded by the Man of Destiny. Indeed, his appointment as Chief of Police of Vienna was a fortune in itself and a fair return for the services he had rendered, and the dangers he had braved as the secret agent of Napoleon.

But Napoleon was not yet satisfied. He wished to be the King of Kings and to reconstruct Germany, Italy and the Netherlands. His ambition was to rule over an empire that should be encircled and guarded by a belt of dependent thrones. In pursuance of this policy he seized Naples and made his brother Joseph its-king. After that he converted the Republic of the Netherlands into a monarchy, and placed his brother Louis at its head with the title of the King of Holland.

In the meantime he needed more information concerning the power and the plans of those who were opposed to his designs. At this stage of events he once more sent for his trusted spy, Schulmeister. He had made him Monsieur de Meinau, with both the title and the estates that went with it. But the new Monsieur knew his imperial patron well enough to understand that he could not rest on his laurels. With Napoleon incessant activity was the price of favor.

As the result of the interview with the Emperor Monsieur left Vienna with letters of introduction to the Austrian officers at Oedenburg. This was in west Hungary, about thirty-seven miles from the Austrian capitol. Here he learned that the Archduke Charles and Ferdinand had combined forces the day before and were preparing for a united attack on the French troops. This information was exceedingly important and he never rested until he had forwarded it to Napoleon.

After that he felt entitled to a little relaxation and he joined the Austrian officers in the gayeties of camp life. He had been hospitably received on his arrival and now was royally entertained by his new found friends. His scarred forehead and his severe military manner impressed them. Add to this the fact that he was supposed to have undergone great privations and dangers as an officer of the Austrian Secret Service and it will not be difficult to understand why the soldiers insisted upon placing a halo of romance around his head. A dinner was given in his honor and on this occasion the rascal actually entertained his hosts

with stories of some of his thrilling adventures in the
service of the Fatherland. His methods were simple
enough. He related real exploits, merely picturing
himself as an Austrian secret agent instead of a spy
of Napoleon. His narratives were received with ap-
plause and manifestations of delight.

The Austrians had been at Oedenburg for some time
and the pleasures of camp life were beginning to affect
the discipline of the men. Schulmeister, or rather
Monsieur de Meinau, was ordinarily a person of ab-
stemious habits, but he could be a jolly good fellow
when the occasion demanded it, and this, you may be
sure, was one of the occasions. The flowing bowl was
passed around so often that it was in grave danger of
flowing over. The more wine the officers drank the
greater became their affection for the spy. They literally threw themselves around his neck, which was
quite a generous thing to do when we consider that
under the military customs of the time they would have
been justified in placing a rope around that same neck.
But there was one man at the banqueting board who
was a death's head at the feast. Lieutenant Bernstein
looked and felt unhappy. He did not share the confidence of his comrades in Monsieur de Meinau. In
fact, he frankly regarded him as a fraud. So he sat
there eating little and drinking less and wondering how
he could bring the spy to grief.

His opportunity came sooner than he expected.
Monsieur de Meinau, having reduced his hosts to a
state of semi-intoxication, hastened out to send further
information to Napoleon. With his usual cleverness

he had established a chain of communication between Oedenburg and Vienna. He had his own sub-spies within and without the lines of the enemy, and thus had a method of forwarding his dispatches which would have been envied by modern news associations in times of war. But on this one occasion he reckoned without his host—or at least this particular host. Bernstein was at his very heels, and when he saw him pass the slips of paper into the hands of a confederate, felt that it was time for some one to interfere. Consequently when Monsieur de Meinau returned to the banqueting board Bernstein pointed an accusing finger in his direction and exclaimed:

"I denounce that man as a spy!"

There was a loud shout of laughter at this and the man nearest to him punched the accuser in the ribs.

"Why, old man, there's nothing startling in that. We know that he is a spy."

Monsieur de Meinau folded his arms and looked the lieutenant in the eye.

"The comrade is trying to have a jest at my expense. Gentlemen, you all know that I am a spy. I have told you myself. Perhaps it was an indiscretion, but—"

"No! No!" cried Bernstein, excitedly. "Not that kind of a spy. I say that he is a spy against Austria. He has been in communication with the French troops. I caught him in the act of sending messages through the lines."

Silence fell upon the group of officers surrounding the two men. The force of the accusation was startling — so startling that it sobered them at once. A bucket of water thrown into each of their faces would not have been half so shocking. All of them turned to Monsieur de Meinau. His face was pale, but he did not lose his composure. He was ready for whatever might happen. The chief officer cried sternly:

" What have you to say to this? "

Monsieur de Meinau's arms were still folded in the way in which he had often seen Napoleon fold his arms.

" Gentlemen," he said with dignity, " I have been grossly insulted, and under the circumstances I can only do one thing — I demand an instant investigation of the accusation against me. I insist upon a trial — a court martial, if you will."

The audacity of this request had the expected result. It disarmed suspicion at the outset. And his insistence upon a trial only served to strengthen him in the minds of the officers. He was given a trial, but it was largely a perfunctory affair. The lieutenant who made the accusation was, of course, unable to prove his charge. The only witnesses against Schulmeister had fled, and he was triumphantly acquitted. He displayed numerous letters, some real and others forged, to prove that he was a patriot working in the Austrian Secret Service. General Wilhing, who presided over the trial, was profuse in his apologies and insisted upon giving him a letter to the Archduke Charles who was then at Koermoend.

Monsieur de Meinau proceeded gayly on his way to

the headquarters of the Archduke, arriving with his letters and his never-failing audacity. His Austrian uniform, of course, was an immense asset, which he did not fail to utilize to the fullest extent. He was not only in the confidence of the Austrians, but also in the position of being a " vindicated " man. Thereafter no one could have the temerity to point the finger of suspicion in his direction. Any charge they might make would have the appearance of being a stale and exploded slander. The most important thing for him now was not to be caught in the commission of any overt act.

Most military spies come to grief by having dispatches and documents on their person. Monsieur de Meinau knew this, and he made it his business to get rid of incriminating documents at the earliest possible moment. But yet there were times when papers and documents were his chief stock in trade. He was cordially received at Koermoend and was taken to the Archduke Charles by a member of that General's staff. The nobleman greeted the newcomer kindly and asked him for information regarding the enemy. Monsieur de Meinau having just come from Vienna via Oedenburg was able to give the Archduke some very interesting news. The fact that the greater part of it was the product of his vivid imagination did not make it any the less thrilling. As a consequence of this the Archduke regarded him with unusual favor.

This fact was not lost on the lesser lights of the camp at Koermoend. The chief-of-staff of the Archduke conceived that one who was so highly regarded

by his superior was entitled to special attention at his
hand.   So he invited him to be his guest during his
brief stay at the headquarters of the Archduke.
Schulmeister — to give him his old name for the moment — accepted cheerfully, but reminded his host that
he was a very busy man and that he might be compelled
at any moment to leave him abruptly and without
notice.   This was the solemn truth, but, of course, the
humor of it was lost on the chief-of-staff.

Now the General had his headquarters in a roomy
frame building not far from that of the Archduke.
His office was in a large apartment on the first floor.
Here he kept all of his papers and military correspondence.   Monsieur de Meinau — to get back to his formal designation — made note of all this and was quick
to see where the soldier placed the keys of the place.
For some days now he followed a policy of watchful
waiting.   He was a persistent man, but also a patient
one.   He felt sure that his opportunity would come —
and it did.

One morning the Archduke decided to make an inspection of his troops.   This was an all-day job and
he was naturally accompanied by his chief-of-staff.
When they were out of sight and hearing the spy
began his operations.   He had access to the house, but
the desk containing the coveted papers was locked.
By rare good — or bad — fortune, the General had
left his bunch of keys on a hook behind the door.
Monsieur de Meinau possessed himself of them and
opened the desk of the absent soldier.   To his delight
he found a mass of most important correspondence.

He tiptoed over to the door and locked it securely. After that he pulled down the blinds and started in to read the papers. It consumed several hours and at the end of that time he had discovered many things which he felt sure were important to Napoleon. The question now was whether to steal the papers or copy them. He finally decided on the latter course. There were two reasons for this. The first was that he could accomplish his purpose without exciting any suspicion and the second that the chief-of-staff, for whom he had come to hold a certain regard, would be held blameless.

He went at his work with a will. He used a cipher of his own which was a sort of shorthand, and long before the sun went down he had filled his memorandum books with most valuable information. Just as he finished there came a loud rapping at the door. He was startled, but not seriously disturbed. He concealed his notebook, locked the desk, placed the keys where he had found them, and then hastily undressed. A couch was in the corner of the room, and he threw himself on it. In the meantime the knocking had become more pronounced. He arose and opened the door, presenting a sleepy and dishevelled appearance to the man at the door. It proved to be, as he had expected, the chief-of-staff, returned from his tour of inspection. Monsieur de Meinau was all apologies.

" I am so sorry to have kept you waiting," he murmured, " but I was tired and I am a heavy sleeper."

The General was graciousness itself.

"No excuses are necessary," he insisted. "I regret having disturbed you. Please lie down again and take the rest I know you must need so badly."

After that speech it might be supposed that Monsieur de Meinau would relent. But not so. He had other uses for his victim. He had supper with him and late that night asked for a safe conduct to Vienna.

"I have to go after some information and it is too late to go to the Archduke. I am sure he would give it to me but I dislike disturbing him. Perhaps it is too much to ask from you?"

The chief-of-staff gave a gracious wave of the arm which might be taken to mean that everything he had was at the disposal of the spy. He said:

"It gives me great pleasure to serve you in this matter because in doing so I know that I am serving my country"

If Monsieur de Meinau had been capable of blushing he would have done so at that moment. But he merely sat there stolidly waiting while the General wrote the desired pass. When it was handed to him he put it in his wallet, bade his host an affectionate farewell and started off with the stolen correspondence.

He reached Vienna in safety and immediately reported to Napoleon, giving the Little Corporal not only the copies of the letters and papers, but also a great amount of verbal information. Napoleon already had his plans made for the campaign which was to end by placing his brother Jerome on the throne of Westphalia. The data given him by Monsieur de Meinau enabled him to dispose his forces still more

advantageously. Also it placed the enemy at a tre-
mendous disadvantage.

At this time there had been formed a new combina-
tion against France, consisting of England, Russia,
Sweden, Saxony and Prussia. The contest began in
1806 with two thrilling battles, Jena and Auerstadt.
They were fought on the same day. It was a crushing
defeat for the Prussians, and Napoleon, already having
possession of Vienna, now marched in triumph into
Berlin. Well might he gloat over his triumph, for he
had accomplished in a few hours what Austria, France
and Russia had been unable to do in the Seven Years'
War of the preceding century. And within a stone's
throw of the Emperor and sharing with him the glories
of this historic occasion was his faithful spy.

But the opposition, while dismayed, was not yet
entirely vanquished. The Prussians gathered their
scattered forces together and joining with the Russians
made a final stand at Eylau. The battle there was
fierce, but not decisive. A short time after this the
French won the battle of Friedland, and then a treaty
of peace was signed.

Napoleon gained precisely what he wanted. By the
peace treaty Prussia gave up a large part of her territory. From a portion of it, lying west of the Elbe,
he created the Kingdom of Westphalia. This was
bestowed upon his brother Jerome, thus adding another
kingdom to the group of states which he was accumu-
lating and which — he thought in his colossal vanity
— was to make him King of Kings. Monsieur de
Meinau was present when Jerome was crowned, as was

befitting for one who had risked his life in the cause of the king-maker.

In 1809 Monsieur de Meinau was given command of the Military Police of the French Army. From that date, although his field of operations was increased, his personal exploits became less numerous. He did undertake one or two private missions for Napoleon, but for the most part his hours were fully occupied in directing the activities of others. That he was a busy man may be appreciated from the ceaseless labors of Napoleon. That remarkable man never rested and, needless to say, did not permit any one about him to rest. There came the seizure of the thrones of Portugal and Spain, the Peninsular War, the quarrel with the Pope, the battle of Wagram and then the divorce from Josephine and the marriage to the Princess Marie Louise. In all of these stirring events the former Alsatian smuggler played his part.

Napoleon, while a hard taskmaster, was a liberal paymaster. Time and again his spy was given large sums of money, and what was quite as good, the opportunities of making money. But there was one thing he craved, and that was the cross of the Legion of Honor. He had been a soldier as well as a spy, and felt that this entitled him to the decoration. Familiar as he had been with the Man of Destiny, the spy did not have the courage to personally ask him for this favor. He confided his wish to General Savery, his original patron, who undertook to present the case to the Emperor. The great Napoleon had ideas of his own on this point. He fully appreciated the value of the services rendered by Schulmeister but when the decoration was demanded he gave an aggressive shake of the head.

"Money as much as you like," he cried, "but the cross — never!"

And the money poured into the outstretched hands· of Monsieur de Meinau, but the decoration of the Legion of Honor remained ever beyond his reach. Presently the fortunes of Napoleon began to wane, and, appropriately enough the fortunes of his chief spy also waned. He became a comparatively poor man and went to spend the declining years of his life in the town of his birth. There Napoleon III called on him and talked of the great days that had gone before.

Some time in the forties a Parisian visiting the Alsatian village met a little old man, dressed in black, and walking about with the aid of a cane. In spite of his great age he was nattily attired and the red rose in his buttonhole betokened the spirit of youth that dwelt within him. He was amiable and very, very gentle. This man was Louis Joseph Schulmeister, afterwards Monsieur de Meinau, Napoleon's chief spy, and the hero of a hundred thrilling escapes.

The good, it is said, die young; this amazing man lived to be eighty-two, and died in bed!

XIII

THE STRANGE MYSTERY SURROUNDING THE BETRAYAL OF CAPTAIN NATHAN HALE

XIII

THE STRANGE MYSTERY SURROUNDING
THE BETRAYAL OF CAPTAIN
NATHAN HALE

MOST Americans are fairly familiar with the story of the heroic sacrifice of Captain Nathan Hale, but none have yet ventured to remove the veil of mystery that hides the identity of the betrayer of the young patriot.

Who delivered Nathan Hale into the hands of his executioners? That is a question which has never been answered. Was it one of his own cousins who happened to be a Tory and a British sympathizer? That suspicion has been expressed and although it has been pushed aside by Benson J. Lossing the historian, he admits that he has not been able to obtain any data for or against this theory.

It is a notorious fact that the Tories were very numerous in and about New York, and there seems to be reason for believing that some of Hale's own family were in sympathy with their sycophantic sentiments. Could feelings of envy have entered into one of the saddest betrayals of American history? It is to be hoped not for the sake of our common humanity, and yet the popularity of Hale as he reached man's estate

189

was likely to arouse the mean jealousy of those of a
lower order of mentality.

Nathan Hale was a magnificent specimen of manhood. His physical and mental qualities were alike
distinguished. He was graduated from Yale college
with high honors and while there made a record as an
athlete. He was almost six feet in height, perfectly
proportioned, and, in the words of Dr. Munson, was
"the most manly man I have ever met." His chest
was broad, his muscles firm; his face wore a most
benign expression; his complexion was rosy; his eyes,
light blue and beaming with intelligence; his hair soft
and light brown and his speech low, sweet and musical.
Is it any wonder that the girls of New Haven loved
him and wept when they heard his fate?

Nathan Hale was engaged in teaching school at New
London when the rumbles of the Revolution first began
to disturb the placid life of that part of the country.
On the day that American blood was first shed at Lexington a twilight town meeting was called and Nathan
Hale was one of the speakers. He called upon the
people to act at once and to act in a manner that could
not be misunderstood.

"Let us march immediately," he cried with all of the
passionate ardor of youth, " and let us never lay down
our arms until we have obtained our independence."

As a proof of both his consistency and his patriotism, Hale immediately enrolled himself as a volunteer.
The following morning he bade good-by to his pupils
and departed for Cambridge. Before long he had
been formally enlisted as a lieutenant of a company in

a regiment commanded by Colonel Charles Webb, and late in September of that year marched with his regiment to Cambridge and participated in the siege of Boston. Within three months he had been commissioned as a captain because of vigilance and bravery. The British were driven from Boston in the spring of the following year, and soon after that the Americans proceeded to New York. His earnestness in the cause was proven when he surrendered his own pay to his men in the endeavor to have them prolong their term of service, which had already expired.

Even at this early stage of his military career he covered himself with glory by performing what proved to be one of the most daring feats of the Revolution. A British sloop laden with provisions was anchored in the East River under the protection of the guns of a man-of-war called the *Asia* Hale went to General Heath and obtained permission to attempt the capture of the supply vessel. With a few dozen picked men as resolute as himself, he embarked in a small boat at midnight and reached the side of the sloop unobserved by the sentinel. The young New Englander followed by his men sprang aboard the vessel; secured the sentinel, confined the crew below the hatches, raised the boat's anchor and took her into the wharf just at the dawn of day. It was a dashing adventure and it was successful. He was the hero of the hour, especially among his fellow Americans, when the supplies were distributed among them. For many months after this he continued the routine work of a captain in the Revolutionary Army, and it was not until the 7th of September that he was called upon to take part in the thrilling exploit which was to end in such a disastrous and tragic manner. Washington had called a council of war to decide whether he should defend or abandon New York. He had already asked Congress this important question and he was answered by a resolution that in case he should find it necessary to quit New York he should have special care taken that no damage be done to the city. As a result of this he resolved to remain and defend the city.

General Washington had at this time made his headquarters at the house of Robert Murray. The position of his army was exceedingly perilous, ships of war having already passed up the East River. Scouts reported great activity among the British troops, but they were unable, after great efforts, to gain any intelligent idea of the intentions of the enemy. Yet Washington knew that it was most essential that he should have this information. He wrote to General Heath, then staying at Kings Bridge.

"As everything in a manner depends upon intelligence of the enemy's motions, I do most earnestly entreat you and General Clinton to exert yourselves to accomplish this most desirable thing. Leave no stone unturned nor do not stick at expense to bring this to pass, as I was never more uneasy than on account of my want of knowledge on this score. Keep a constant lookout with good glasses on some commanding heights that look well on to the other shore."

What Washington desired to know more than anything else was whether the British would make a direct attack upon the city, and if they did whether they intended to land upon the island above the city or Morrisania, beyond the Harlem River.   The general in his perplexity called another council of war at Murray's. At this conference it was resolved to send some courageous and competent person in disguise into the British camps on Long Island.   The person needed was one skilled in military and scientific knowledge and a good draftsman — in short a man on whose judgment and fidelity they could absolutely depend.   In this emergency Washington sent for Lieutenant Colonel Noulton and told him just what he wanted.   In response Noulton summoned a number of officers to a conference at his quarters and in the name of the commander-in-chief called for volunteers.   They were taken by surprise.   There was a general reluctance to engage in the work of a spy.   For a time it looked as if it would be impossible to obtain a man for the service, but at the last moment a young soldier who had been ill entered the room and learning the nature of the request called out:

" I will undertake the work."

It was Captain Nathan Hale.   Everybody was amazed, not the least among them being Lieutenant Colonel Noulton.   Some of the others, who knew and loved Hale, privately endeavored to persuade him to reconsider his decision.   They pointed out his hopes for the future and explained the ignominy and death to which he might be exposed.   One of his dearest friends, William Hull, who was afterwards a general in the War of 1812, and who was a member of his

company and had been his classmate at college, was
especially fervid in trying to turn him from the perilous
task, but Hale had made up his mind and would not
change it. He said with great warmth:

"Gentlemen, I am satisfied that I owe to my country the accomplishment of an object so important and
so much desired by the commander of her armies, and
I know of no mode of obtaining the information except
by assuming a disguise and passing into the enemy's
camp. I am fully sensible of the consequences of discovery and capture in such circumstances, but for a
year I have been attached to the army and have not
rendered any material service, while receiving a compensation for which I made no return. Yet I am not
influenced by any expectation of promotion or pecun-
iary reward. I wish to be useful; and every kind of
service necessary for the public good becomes honorable by being necessary. If the exigencies of my country demand a peculiar service its claims to the perform-
ance of that service are imperious."

These words, thrilling with their patriotism, silenced
the objections of his fellow soldiers. That very afternoon in company with Noulton he appeared before
Washington and received instructions concerning his
mission. He was provided with the necessary authority and also given a general order to the owners of all
American vessels to convey him to any point on Long
Island which he might designate.

He left the camp on Harlem Heights that night
accompanied by Sergeant Stephen Hempstead. With
him also was his servant, Ansel Wright. It was not

until they had reached Norwalk, fifty miles from New York, that they found a safe place to cross the Sound. Here Hale exchanged his regimentals for citizen's dress of brown cloth and a broad brimmed round hat. He directed his two companions to remain there until his return and also deposited with Hempstead his uniform and his military commission. Hale crossed the Sound to Huntingdon Bay where he landed disguised in the character of schoolmaster and Royalist who was disgusted with the Rebel forces. He entered the British camps in this disguise and was received with much enthusiasm by the Redcoats, who accepted him as an ally. It is known that he visited all the British camps on Long Island and made observations openly; that he passed over from Brooklyn to New York City and that he gathered considerable information concerning the condition of the British army at that place. So far he had been entirely successful in his mission.

On his return he safely reached the point on the Long Island shore where he had first landed, and he prepared to recross the Sound at Norwalk the first thing in the following morning. He wore shoes with loose inner soles and between the soles he had concealed the drawings he made of the fortifications and also other memoranda written in Latin on thin paper. Perfectly satisfied that he was safe from harm and filled with the thought that his mission had ended successfully, he calmly awaited the coming of daylight. His attention was attracted by the proximity of an inn known as " The Cedars." This place was managed by a widow who was a staunch Loyalist. It was well

known as the resort of the Tories in that part of
the country.   Hale was familiar with these facts, but
was not disturbed at the thought of any personal
danger.

The light in the window of " The Cedars " attracted
him.   It was necessary that he should have refreshments and lodgings.   He felt perfectly safe now, con-
sidering that he was far away from the danger zone,
and besides felt that his simple attire would protect
him from prying eyes.   Accordingly he strolled into
the tavern and secured a room for the night.   After
that he went to the main room and ordered supper.
The place was fairly crowded and the entrance of Hale
apparently attracted no attention.

He took his ease, supping leisurely and listening with
interest to the gossip of the loungers about the room.
" The Cedars " was notoriously a resort for Tories and
the young American was forced to listen to some conversation which he surely did not relish.   But he had
a sense of humor as well as a philosophy of his own
and the blatant talk of the so-called Royalists did not
disturb the serenity of his disposition.   Indeed, there
is reason to believe that the romantic side of the young
man was attracted by the novelty of the situation.
" The Cedars " was a quaint old inn.   The customary
shingle, offering refreshments for " man and beast "
swung outside in the wind; mine host with a long white
apron served beer in great stone mugs, and the patrons
of the place sprawled about the tables smoking long
stemmed pipes.   They talked of war and they talked
of spies, little thinking that an American officer who

was just finishing an important mission was listening to all they had to say.

In the midst of the hub-bub a stranger entered the room. He caught one glance of Nathan Hale and then turned his face with the suddenness of one who has made a startling discovery. The next moment Hale had looked up, but too late to get a good view of the man's face. He caught the merest glance of the guilty countenance, and from that moment his mind was haunted with a resemblance which it was impossible to fix with any certainty. The newcomer was in civilian's dress. He wore his hair long and was square-shouldered. He spoke to no one and disappeared as silently as he had entered.

There can be no doubt that he is the man who betrayed Hale to the British. But there has always been real doubt concerning his identity. It is hinted that Hale himself said that the fellow resembled a distant cousin. But there is nothing on record to prove this disagreeable suspicion. Indeed, from that moment, there seems to have been an attempt to conceal all of the facts concerning Hale's dramatic arrest and tragic death. Can this have been part of the plan to protect the informer? Over one hundred and forty years have passed since then and history still asks the name of the man who entered " The Cedars " on that fateful night in September, 1775.

Nathan Hale spent the night at this tavern, and at daylight the next morning he went out to search for the boat that was to convey him to the other side of the Sound. To his immense satisfaction he saw a craft

moving towards the shore with several men in it. He
had not the least doubt but that they were his friends
and he hastened to the beach in order to meet it. As
the boat touched the shore a half dozen British marines
jumped out and surrounded him. He turned as if to
run when a harsh voice exclaimed:

" Surrender instantly, or you die ! "

Too late he realized that he had walked into a trap.
He saw six men standing there erect with muskets
levelled at his heart. It was folly to struggle. He
was seized, taken into the barge and conveyed to the
British guardship *Halifax*. His captors stripped and
searched him and found the evidence of his mission
concealed between the soles of his shoes. The unfortunate American was taken in one of the boats of the
Halifax to General Howe's headquarters, which were
then in the mansion of James Beekman at Mount
Pleasant. This place contained among other things a
great greenhouse filled with shrubbery and plants. In
this greenhouse Hale was confined under a strong
guard on the night of September 21. The following
morning he was taken before Howe, who, without the
formality of a trial, condemned him to be hung. He
was delivered into the custody of William Cunningham with orders that he should be executed before sunrise the following day.

History informs us that when Hale was taken before
Howe he frankly acknowledged the purpose of his
mission.

" I was present at the interview," wrote a British
officer, " and I observed that the frankness, the manly

bearing and the evident disinterested patriotism of the young prisoner touched a tender cord in General Howe's nature; but the stern rules of war concerning such offenses would not allow him to exercise even pity."

It was on a Sunday morning that Nathan Hale was marched to the place of execution, which was in the vicinity of what is now East Broadway and Market Street. He was escorted by a file of soldiers and was permitted to sit in a tent while waiting for the necessary preparations for his death. The young patriot asked for a chaplain but his request was brutally denied. He asked for a Bible, but this also was refused. It was only at the solicitation of a young officer in whose tent Hale sat that he was allowed to write brief letters to his mother, sisters and the young girl to whom he was betrothed. She was Alice Adams, a native of Canterbury, Connecticut, and distinguished both for her intelligence and personal beauty. Who could imagine the feelings that filled the young patriot as he penned his final words to the girl who was pledged to be his wife.

But imagine the scene a moment later when these tender epistles were handed to Cunningham. That officer read them with growing anger. He became furious as he realized the noble spirit which breathed in every word. He resolved that they should not be given to the world, and with an oath tore them into bits before the face of his victim. It was twilight on that beautiful September morning when Hale was led to his execution. The gallows was the limb of an apple tree in Colonel Rutger's orchard. The young martyr was asked if he had anything to say. He turned to his executioner and in a calm clear voice said:

"I only regret that I have but one life to lose for my country."

His body was buried near the spot where he died and a British officer was sent to acquaint Washington with the fate of his young messenger. A rude stone placed by the side of the grave of his father in the burial ground of the Congregational Church in his native town for many years revealed to passersby the fact that it was "In Commemoration of Nathan Hale, Esquire, a Captain in the Army of the United States, who was Born June Sixth, 1755, and Received the First Honors of Yale College, September 17, 1773, and Resigned His Life a Sacrifice to His Country's Liberty at New York, September 22, 1776, Age Twenty-two."

Sixty years ago, long before there was a monument to the memory of Hale, George Gibbs, librarian of the New York Historical Society, wrote this epitaph, which is worthy of preservation:

STRANGER, BENEATH THIS STONE
LIES THE DUST OF
A SPY,
WHO PERISHED UPON THE GIBBET;
YET
THE STORIED MARBLES OF THE GREAT,
THE SHRINES OF HEROES,
ENTOMBED ONE NOT MORE WORTHY OF
HONOR

Nathan Hale.

THAN HIM WHO HERE
SLEEPS HIS LAST SLEEP.
NATIONS
BOW WITH REVERENCE BEFORE THE DUST
OF HIM WHO DIES
A GLORIOUS DEATH,
URGED ON BY THE SOUND OF THE
TRUMPET
AND THE SHOUTS OF
ADMIRING THOUSANDS
BUT WHAT REVERENCE, WHAT HONOR,
IS NOT DUE TO ONE,
WHO FOR HIS COUNTRY ENCOUNTERED
EVEN AN INFAMOUS DEATH,
SOOTHED BY NO SYMPATHY,
ANIMATED BY NO PRAISE!

The simple narrative of Nathan Hale's life and death effectively disposes of the tradition that he undertook his perilous mission reluctantly or that he had any scruples about essaying the rôle of a spy. He regarded that task as part of the day's work — an unpleasant part to be sure, but one of the things that had to be cheerfully undertaken in the line of duty.

But there is one phase of the tragic business that is shrouded in mystery and it is the story of his betrayal. Who was the strange man in " The Cedars " ? Was he a cousin? Was he a Tory? Do the descendants of that man still live in New York City and what must their feelings be when they read the inscription upon the monument to the young patriot and martyr?

Until these questions have been answered and until this mystery has been made clear the story of Nathan Hale will be incomplete.

XIV

MAJOR LE CARON AND THE FENIAN
INVASION OF CANADA

XIV

MAJOR LE CARON AND THE FENIAN
INVASION OF CANADA

IF there is one name in Ireland that is more cordially detested than another it is that of Thomas Beach, the spy, who is better known by his adopted name of Major Henri Le Caron.   The story of how he came to assume that cognomen, and the manner in which he served the government of Great Britain as against his supposed co-patriots furnishes one of the most interesting chapters in the Secret Service of England, if not of the world.

Beach defends his work on the ground that when he was first brought into contact with Fenianism he had no ulterior motive in mind and that no material consideration prompted him to work against the men who hoped to bring about the freedom of Ireland by the spectacular invasion of Canada.   He says that he was forced by a variety of circumstances to play a part he had never sought, but he insists that he did nothing to be ashamed of and has never felt any regret for the manner in which he served England.   He says that there is no truth in the popular belief which credited him with receiving fabulous payments and frequent rewards.   He admits that there was ever-present danger and constantly recurring difficulties, but very scant recompense from the Government for which he risked so much.

Beach was born in England, but came to the United States just about the time of the beginning of the Civil War and enlisted in the Union Army — in the 8th Pennsylvanian Reserves. But in enlisting he took on himself a new name and a new nationality. One reason he gives for this was his desire to avoid giving his parents anxiety. Also he thought it would be "a good joke." Be that as it may, he was put down on the books of his company as Henri Le Caron and his home as France. He served through the greater part of the war, and after it was over became connected with the Grand Army of the Republic, holding among other positions those of Vice Commander and Post Surgeon, with the rank of major.

So from that time until the end of the chapter he was known as Major Le Caron, and he says that this afforded him an effective disguise through which he was enabled to keep the English authorities informed of the Irish movements on this side of the Atlantic.

It was through an Irishman named O'Neill that Le Caron became connected with the Fenian movement. He wrote home at intervals and he says that the information which was thus informally given to his family was by them taken to the Home Secretary in London, and in the course of time Le Caron became a regularly paid spy in the Secret Service. The consequences of this was that the proposed invasion of Canada was well known to the English and Canadian officials long before it occurred. The first invasion, with which

MAJOR LE CARON (THOMAS BEACH)

Le Caron does not seem to have been personally connected occurred on the morning of June 1, 1866.   For
six months before that time active preparations were in
progress.   During the spring of the year many com-
panies of soldiers, armed and uniformed, were being
drilled in a number of cities in the United States.
Thousands of stands of arms and millions of rounds of
ammunition had been purchased and located at different points along the Canadian border.

The relations between the United States and England were not very cordial at that time because of the
attitude of England during the Civil War, and as a
consequence the proposed invasion, if it was not encouraged, was not greatly discouraged in this country.
The attempt, however, proved a failure.   The Fenians
were defeated and driven out of Canada.   Sixty of
them were killed and more than two hundred taken
prisoners.   It was the natural result that is to be looked
for when a volunteer force goes against a well trained
army.   Under the command of General John O'Neill
800 Irish patriots were towed across the Niagara River
to a point on the Canadian side called Waterloo.   At
four o'clock in the morning the Irish flag was planted
on British soil by Colonel Owen Starr, and from thence
the patriots marched to and captured Fort Erie, containing a detachment of the Welland Battery.

The effect of the news of this first victory was elec-
trical in the United States.   Thousands who had hesitated about joining the movement were now willing
and anxious to enlist.   The Canadian Government,
and Le Caron in his official reports to London endeav-

ored to belittle this initial triumph, but they felt very much chagrined just the same. However, the Irish victory was short-lived. As soon as the news of the capture of Fort Erie spread to Toronto, the 22nd Battalion of Volunteers of that city hastened to the rescue, and at Ridgeway a bloody battle occurred between the opposing forces. The invaders were driven back to Fort Erie and later were taken as prisoners by the United States battleship *Michigan.*

The news of the temporary victory had a wonderful effect in the United States. By the 7th of June not less than 30,000 men had assembled in and around Buffalo, prepared to fight if it was deemed desirable. But the defeat of the detachment that had actually entered Canada, and the issuance of a neutrality proclamation by President Andrew Johnson ended the war for the time being. The prisoners were released on their own recognizance and sent home by the United States authorities. The arms seized by the American Government were returned to the Fenian organization, and if Dame Rumor is not a falsifier, were used for a second invasion of Canada four years later.

In 1869 Le Caron was so intimate with his Fenian friends that he was made an inspector general of the Irish Republican Army. After that he was assistant adjutant general with the rank of colonel, and his new position enabled him not only to become possessed of the originals of many important documents and plans of proposed campaigns, but also specimens of the Fenian army commissions which he promptly conveyed to the officials of the Canadian Government. In this work he was assisted by a number of officials from Canada. Speaking of this, he says:

"Successful as I was in avoiding detection through all this work, those assisting me in my secret service capacity were not always destined to share in my good luck. This has been particularly the case on one occasion. I was at the time shipping arms at Malone, N. Y., and attended on behalf of the Canadian Government by one of the staff men placed at my disposal for the purpose of immediate communication and the transit of any documents requiring secrecy and dispatch as well as for personal protection should such prove necessary. This man, John C. Rose, was one of the most faithful and trusted servants of the Canadian administration, and for months he followed me along the whole border.

"Though stopping at the same hotels and in constant communication with me, no suspicion was aroused until his identity was accidentally disclosed by a visitor from the seat of government to one of the Fenians located at Malone. Men were immediately set to watch him without my knowledge, and the fact of his being found always in my wake on my visits to and from several towns led to the belief that he was spying upon my actions. A few nights after this poor Rose on his return from sending a dispatch from the post-office, was waylaid, robbed and brutally beaten, and subsequently brought back to the hotel in as sorry a plight as I ever saw."

In the meantime, in the winter of 1869, the Fenian Senate announced the completion of the arrangements for the invasion of Canada, and early in February of the following year circulars were sent out to the military officers of the Fenian Brotherhood, instructing them to prepare for the proposed campaign. Those Brothers whose business or family duties prevented them from getting their commands in readiness for active and immediate service were requested to forward their resignations at once and at the same time send on the names of persons suitable to take their places. They were told to ascertain and report how many of their own men could furnish their own transportation, and in the meantime to try and persuade all of them to save enough for that purpose.

On Saturday, April 22, 1870, General O'Neill and Le Caron left Buffalo for St. Albans, the general being filled with enthusiasm over the belief that the Canadians would be taken entirely by surprise, and Le Caron laughing in his sleeve at the thought of how his companion would be fooled. O'Neill's plan was to get across the boundary line without delay and then to entrench himself at a point where his soldiers would form the nucleus around which a large army and unlimited support would rally from the United States. Buffalo, Malone, and Franklin were the three points from which attacks were to be made. O'Neill expected 1,000 men to meet him at Franklin, on the night of April 25, 1870. Only a quarter of that number presented themselves, and by the following morning not more than 500 had mustered. Every hour's delay added to the danger of failure and collapse. All this time Le Caron was busy sending messages across

the border carrying full details as to the time the Fenians would leave Franklin, the exact points at which
they would cross the border, their numbers, and the
places of their contemplated operation.

On April 26 O'Neill left the Franklin Hotel to place
himself at the head of the Fenian Army. Hubbard's
Farm, the Fenian camp and rendezvous, was about
half a mile from Franklin, and here all of the available
soldiers had been mustered. Arranging them in line,
O'Neill, according to Le Caron's narrative, addressed
them as follows:

" Soldiers, this is the advance guard of the Irish-
American army for the liberation of Ireland from
the yoke of the oppressor. For the sake of your
own country you enter that of the enemy. The
eyes of your countrymen are upon you. Forward,
march! "

Following this harangue they started off on their
expedition with O'Neill at their head. Before leaving,
O'Neill instructed Le Caron to bring to his support
on their arrival a party of 400 men who were coming
from St. Albans. The men marched with a certain
amount of military precision for all of them had
received some degree of military training. There is
no doubt of the patriotic feelings that filled their
hearts. In spite of the lack of uniformity, and possibly because of it, the scene was picturesque. Here and
there a Fenian coat with its green and gray faced with
gold sparkled in contrast with the civilian clothing
and the more somber garb of the others.

Finally the volunteers reached a little wooden bridge

and deployed as skirmishers in close order, advancing with fixed bayonets and cheering wildly. Not a soldier appeared to dispute their way, but the dark Canadian trees hid from their view the ambushed Canadian volunteers, who were only awaiting the signal to spring out upon the unsuspecting invaders.

All this time Le Caron, who had spent years of intimate association with many of the Irishmen and who was regarded as their friend and confidant, stood upon the hilltop to watch the inevitable slaughter. They advanced a few yards farther, and on their startled ears came the whistling sound of many bullets from the rifles of the ambushed Canadians as they poured a deadly volley straight into their ranks.

Little remains to be told. There was fierce fighting and terrible bloodshed, but the invaders were overcome by superior numbers and well disciplined troops. Finally they were forced to retreat up to the hill where Le Caron stood, still under the fire of their adversaries and leaving their dead to be subsequently buried by the Canadians.

Seeing that all was over, for the time at least, the spy had hurried off to the point where the St. Albans contingent had arrived and were forming. He actually took part in this ceremony, and while engaged in superintending it he was afforded, as he says, practical evidence of the termination of O'Neill's part in the fight. While he was standing in the middle of the road where the men were forming into line, he was startled by the cry:

" Clear the road, clear the road! "

He was almost knocked down by a team of horses pulling a covered carriage, and as the conveyance flashed by him he caught through the carriage window a hurried glimpse of the dejected face of General O'Neill, who was seated between two men. He said in speaking of this that he might have given the command to shoot the horses as they turned an adjacent corner, but it was no part of his purpose to restore O'Neill to his command.

It became known later that O'Neill was in the custody of the United States Marshal, General Foster, who, acting under instructions from Washington, had arrived on the scene of the battle immediately after Le Caron left and arrested O'Neill on the charge of breaking the neutrality laws. O'Neill, who was in the company of his comrades, refused to surrender and threatened force, but when General Foster placed a revolver at his head he succumbed.

Late that afternoon when the news of O'Neill's arrest became known, a council of war was held, presided over by John Boyle O'Reilly: On the following morning General Spear, the secretary of war of the Fenian Brotherhood, arrived at St. Albans and tried to do something practical in the way of continuing the invasion. He pleaded with Le Caron to supply him with 400 or 500 stands of arms and ammunition within the next twenty-four hours, but the spy felt that it would not do for him to allow further operations, and so he said that it would be impossible to grant the demands under the condition of affairs then prevailing. Thousands of Canadian troops had arrived on the bor-

der and were making the position of the Irish volunteers more precarious every moment.

Fortunately for Le Caron, the appearance of United
States troops in the vicinity put any further attempt at
war operations out of the question, for in order to
avoid arrest for a breach of the neutrality laws the
Fenians were compelled to disappear. The spy left
with them and hurried to Malone and found a similar
state of affairs prevailing there, although the arrest of
O'Neill and the anticipated appearance of United
States troops filled the invaders with dismay.

Le Caron was elated with his success and anxious to
report himself at the Canadian headquarters without
delay. He knew, however, that it would not be safe
for him to go direct to Ottawa so he traveled in a
roundabout way. One night he stopped with the Com-
missioner of the Quebec police, and the following
morning took a train for Ottawa. Before this journey was concluded he found that he had been altogether too premature in his self congratulations,
because that journey brought him closer to discovery
than he had ever been before.

The incident which threatened to deprive him of his
usefulness as a spy occurred at Cornwall where there
was the usual half hour's delay for dinner. He was
in the midst of his meal, enjoying it with great zest in
spite of the fact that his work as a spy had sent hundreds of men to their death, when two men stopped and
gazed at him with unusual interest. One of them was
tall and very military in his manner, and the other
had on clerical attire. As Le Caron ceased eating he

heard the clerical looking one say as he pointed his finger in his direction:

"That is the man!"

Advancing, the tall man, who subsequently turned out to be the Mayor of Cornwall, said with a Scotch accent:

"You are my prisoner!"

These words were accompanied with a strong grasp of the hand on the shoulder of the suspected one. He imagined there was some mistake, and laughed as he turned around to resume his dinner, but the Scotchman gave an added squeeze to his arm as he solemnly repeated the words:

"You are my prisoner, and you must go with me at once."

It turned out later that the ministerial looking person was a wandering preacher who happened to be in the vicinity of Malone when Le Caron was loading arms there and he had been pointed out to him as the leading Fenian agent. The preacher's memory was a very good one, and he immediately recognized the spy when he met him again.

It was a serious condition of affairs for Le Caron, but still he could not entirely comprehend what it all meant, and he said:

"Will not you let me finish my dinner?"

"No," was the sharp reply, "you have got to come at once."

"For what reason am I arrested?" asked Le Caron.

"You are a Fenian," was the indignant reply, and then for the first time the spy noticed that the crowd in the room was beginning to show signs of anger and indignation toward him.

He was hurried out by his captors and taken to a room adjoining the ticket office, where a demand was made on him for his luggage and keys with everything on his person. He had with him documents which would reveal everything if they were made public. His position was dangerous, as he puts it "distinctly dangerous."

In this emergency he asked the Mayor for a few minutes' private conversation, and it was accorded him. They went inside the ticket office and Le Caron told him the exact situation. It was true, he admitted, that he had been working with the Fenians, but he was also a Government agent. In fact he was a British spy who had been keeping the Canadian officials informed of the details of the proposed invasion. He said that he was then on his way to Ottawa to see Judge McMicken. He said that to delay or expose him would mean serious difficulty to the Government.

His manner must have impressed the Mayor, for he decided to send him on to Ottawa in charge of an escort with instructions to find out from Judge McMicken whether his story was to be believed. The details of Le Caron's arrest as a Fenian quickly spread amongst his fellow passengers and the reception he received along the journey was not very agreeable, so for safety's sake the lieutenant transferred him to the care of a sergeant and two other soldiers. The carriage in which they traveled was the sole point of attraction in the train, and the Canadians, crowding around this carriage, hissed and hooted him, while their cries of " Hang him!   Lynch him! " gave him a very uncomfortable idea of what would happen if he were left alone amongst them.

On reaching Prescott junction Le Caron found the news of his capture had preceded him and created such a sensation that a special correspondent of the *Toronto Globe* had traveled to meet him in order to find out who and what he was and everything about him.   The spy of course refused to have anything to say.   When the party arrived at Ottawa a representative of Judge McMicken was waiting for him at the station.   He was conveyed to the police station without delay, and there the judge heard the details of his capture and received possession of his person and gave a formal receipt for his custody.   After the guard left the judge listened to the recital of the spy and arranged that his identity should not become public.   He also supplied him with needful funds to leave Canada.   This came in the form of a check and it was necessary to have some one cash it.   This was done at one of the clubs in Ottawa and the amount of the check — $350.00 — caused the club porter to speak of it to some of his friends.   This porter knew that Le Caron was the Fenian prisoner and he let out the secret a little later. It became public property and the Canadian press published the fact that an important Fenian had been in Ottawa immediately after the raid and received a large sum of money from a Government official with whom he was in communication, adding that the Fenians must have been nicely duped all through.

218 THE WORLD'S GREATEST SPIES

Le Caron was very much disturbed by this publication. It was bringing danger very close to him, and yet strange as it may appear, suspicion did not rest upon him in connection with the newspaper story. He drove from Ottawa in the night and got safely home, not being troubled afterwards by any of the events of that fateful invasion into Canada.

Le Caron studied medicine after that and subsequently became connected with the Clan-na-Gael. He became one of the members of the military board of organization and in that capacity continued to send information to his friends at Scotland Yard. While he was in this organization he became acquainted with many of its leading members who believed that he was really a friend of Ireland and who never suspected that he was connected with the British Government and was regularly receiving compensation for the information which he sent from time to time to the home office in London.

Le Caron continued to serve as an English spy for nearly twenty years after the Fenian invasion of Canada. His part in that affair — or at least the part he played in keeping the Canadian and English governments informed of the movements of the Irish patriots — was never suspected by the men with whom he was associated and with whom he lived on such intimate terms. He was in constant communication with Mr. Anderson, the head of Scotland Yard, and his letters to that official, if gathered together, would make a volume in themselves. On one occasion when he was leaving America for a trip abroad he was entrusted with letters to Patrick Egan and other Irish leaders. He met Egan in Paris, and spent weeks with him in visiting places of interest in the French capital. They attended the theater together and dined at various restaurants in company, and Le Caron proudly boasts that he never had to spend a penny, because Egan insisted upon being the host at their various entertainments.

But it was when the famous suit of Parnell against the *London Times* was tried that the spy was at last revealed in his true light. He says of that event:

"On Tuesday morning, the 5th of February, 1889, the curtain was rung up, and throwing aside the mask forever, I stepped into the witness box and came out in my true colors, as an Englishman, proud of his country, and in no sense ashamed of his record in her services."

His one complaint was that he had been treated badly in the matter of his pay by the British Government. He said that "the miserable pittance doled out for the purpose of fighting the Clan-na-Gael becomes perfectly ludicrous" in the light of the service he was called on to perform.

It all depends upon the way in which the business is regarded, and there are still a great many persons that will resent the effort of Thomas Beach, or Major Henri Le Caron, to place a halo about his head.

XV

HOW EMMA EDMONDS PENETRATED
THE CONFEDERATE LINES

XV

HOW EMMA EDMONDS PENETRATED
THE CONFEDERATE LINES

THIS is a leaf from the life of an extraordinary woman who served as a nurse and a spy in the Union army during the Civil War in the United States, and who was a pronounced success in both capacities. Few women that have passed through such thrilling adventures are so little known to fame, yet if the patient seeker be willing to spare the time and the labor he may find in the files of the War Department at Washington reports in her handwriting which had a material influence upon more than one battle during the four years of the war.

Emma Edmonds was an adopted American. She was born and educated in the province of New Brunswick, but came to the United States at an early age. She was passing through New York on her way to her future home in New England when the newspapers appeared on the street with the announcement of the fall of Fort Sumter, and President Lincoln's call for seventy-five thousand men. That happening changed the entire course of her life. Ten days later she had been enrolled as a field nurse in the Union army, and was in Washington waiting to be detailed for duty.

The first assignment came sooner than was expected.

Almost before she knew it she was in the thick of the work that followed the battle of Manassas. She spent three hours with other nurses in caring for the needs of the men — even while the battle was in progress. Presently the enemy made a desperate charge on the Union troops, driving them back and taking possession of the spring from which they obtained their water. The chaplain's horse was shot from under him and bled to death in a little while. Not long afterwards Colonel Cameron, brother of the Secretary of War, came dashing along the line shouting:

" Come on, boys, they're in full retreat! "

The words had scarcely been uttered when he fell, pierced to the heart by a bullet. It was mortal and all that the nurse could do was to fold his arms, close his eyes and leave him in the cold embrace of death. And all the while the battle raged about them. This was but one of a score of incidents that prepared a frail woman for the breath-taking career which she was to follow during the four years of the Civil War — incidents which are more thrilling than those to be found in the pages of the most exciting fiction.

All of this was preliminary to Emma Edmonds' work as a spy. One morning a detachment of the Thirty-seventh New York Regiment that had been sent out on scouting duty returned with several prisoners and the statement that one of the Federal spies had been captured and executed. There was regret, not alone over the death of the man, but also because a valuable soldier had been lost to the United States Secret Service. Incidentally it brought the opportunity for which the fearless woman had been waiting. She was told that she might have the opportunity of becoming a spy if she fully realized the danger and the responsibility that was attached to the post. She considered it carefully and said that if appointed she would accept and do the best she knew how for the Government.

Her name was sent to headquarters, and she was soon summoned to appear there herself. She was questioned and cross-questioned at some length; she was examined at length as to her knowledge of fire-arms, and finally the oath of allegiance was administered and she became a regular commissioned spy for the Federal army. It was at once decided that she should adopt a disguise and attempt to penetrate the Confederate lines.

In the first place she purchased a suit of contraband clothing, real plantation style such as the male negroes wore, and then went to a barber and had her hair sheared close to her head. After that, by the use of stains and dyes she colored her face, and then she was ready for business. It might be well to state, at this stage of the narrative, that Emma Edmonds while in the secret service penetrated the enemy's lines, in various disguises, no less than eleven times; always with complete success and without detection.

She started on her first expedition toward the Confederate capitol with the greatest confidence imaginable. With a few hard crackers in her pocket and her revolver loaded and capped she began the journey on foot, and without a blanket or any other kind of baggage that might excite suspicion. At half-past nine o'clock at night she passed the outer picket line of the Union army and at twelve o'clock was within the Confederate lines without once being halted by a sentinel. Once she passed within ten rods of a Confederate picket without being detected.

As soon as she had gone a safe distance from the picket lines she lay down and rested until morning. The night was chilly and the ground damp and she passed the weary hours in fear and trembling. The first thing in the morning she met a party of negroes carrying hot coffee and provisions to the Confederate pickets. This was most fortunate for she made their acquaintance, and after securing a hot breakfast she marched into Yorktown with them without eliciting the slightest suspicion. The negroes went to work at once on fortifications that were being erected, and the spy was left by herself. But an officer seeing her a few minutes later turned to an overseer and said:

" Take that black rascal and set him to work, and if he don't work well tie him up and give him twenty lashes."

So saying he rode away, and the disguised one was conducted to a breastwork which was in course of erection and where there were about a hundred negroes at work. She was soon furnished with a pick and shovel and a wheelbarrow and put to work. It was hard — hard enough for the strongest man, but with occasional assistance from some kind-hearted darky she managed to do her part. All day long she worked in this manner until her hands were blistered and her back nearly broken. When night came she was released from her toil and was free to go where she pleased. She made good use of her liberty. She wandered about the place and made out a brief report of the mounted guns she found in her ramble around the fort. There were fifteen three-inch rifle cannon, eighteen four and a half inch rifle cannon, twenty-nine thirty-two pounders, twenty-three eight-inch Columbiads, eleven nine-inch Dalgrens, thirteen ten-inch Columbiads, fourteen ten-inch mortars and seven eight-inch siege howitzers.

This capitulation must sound strange to those acquainted with present-day methods of warfare, but it was all very important to the spy, who made out her list with the greatest care. After that she made a rough sketch of the outer works, and placing the precious papers under the inner sole of her contraband shoe she returned to the negro quarters. She did not want to stay with them, but she did wish to find some one among them who would change places with her on the following day. She was fortunate in discovering a lad of about her own size who was engaged in carrying water to the troops. He said he would take her place next day and he thought he could find a friend to do the same thing the following day, for which evidence of brotherly kindness the female spy offered him $5.00 in greenbacks, which, he said, was more money than he had ever seen in all of his life before. By this arrangement Miss Edmonds escaped the scrutiny of the overseer, who might have detected her disguise.

The second day in the Confederate service was pleasanter than the first. She had only to supply one brigade with water, which did not require much energy, for the day was cool and the well not far distant. As a result of this she had an opportunity of lounging among the soldiers and of hearing important steps discussed. In this way she learned the number of reënforcements which had arrived from different places and also had the pleasure of seeing General Lee, who came there to consult with other Confederates. It was whispered among the men that he had been telegraphed to for the purpose of inspecting the fortifications, as he was the best engineer in the Confederacy and that he had pronounced it impossible to hold Yorktown after McClellan opened his siege guns upon it. General Johnson was hourly expected with a force at his command, and including all, the Confederates estimated their force in and around Yorktown at 150,000 men.

When General Johnson arrived a council of war was held. Soon after that the report began to circulate that the town was to be evacuated. It was at this stage of the game that Miss Edmonds saw a man who had been coming into the Federal camp as a peddler of newspapers and stationery, and now here he was giving the Confederates a full description of the Union camp and the Union forces. She watched him closely and discovered him displaying a map of the entire works of McClellan's position.

Miss Edmonds decided that it was of the utmost importance for her to leave the camp of the enemy and carry the information she possessed to the Union headquarters. The important thing now was to leave

without being detected. On the evening of the third
day from the time she entered the camp of the enemy
she was sent in company with colored men to carry
supper to the outer picket posts. This was just what
she hoped and wished for. During the day she had
provided herself with a canteen of whisky. Some of
the men on picket duty were colored and others were
white, but calling them to her side she spread before
them corn cake and added to that a moderate amount
of whisky for dessert. While they were thus engaged
minnie balls were whistling around their heads, for the
picket lines of the two armies were not more than half
a mile distant from each other.

Not long after nightfall an officer came riding along
the lines, and seeing the spy there, wanted to know his
business. One of the darkies replied that she had
helped to carry out their supper and was waiting until
the Yankees stopped firing before she started back.
Turning to the disguised one, he said:

"You come along with me. I'll see that you have
something to occupy your mind."

Miss Edmonds did as she was ordered and they went
back the way he had come until they had gone about
fifty rods, then halting in front of a petty officer he
said:

"Put this fellow on the post where that man was
shot — and see that he stays there until I return."

So the spy was conducted a few rods farther and
then a rifle put in her hands, which she was told to use
freely in case she should see anybody or anything
approaching from the enemy. The officer, of course,

regarded her as an irresponsible negro, and after giving her the assignment took her by the coat collar and gave her a vigorous shake.

"Now, you black rascal," he cried, "if I catch you sleeping at your post I'll shoot you like a dog."

It was a startling position for a stranger in a strange land, especially when that one happened to be a female spy in disguise. The night was very dark and it was beginning to rain. She was all alone now and she could not guess when she would be relieved or just what the next hour might bring forth. Her one thought was to escape. After ascertaining as well as possible the position of the picket on each side of her — each of whom was enjoying the shelter of the nearest tree — she deliberately and noiselessly stepped into the darkness and was soon gliding swiftly through the forest toward the Union lines. She had to make her approach very carefully for she was in as much danger of being shot by her friends as by the enemy, so she spent the remainder of the night within hailing distance of the Union lines, and with the first dawn of morning hoisted the well known signal and was heartily welcomed back to her own camp.

She made her way to the tent containing the hospital nurses and removed as much of the color from her face as was possible with the aid of soap and water. She then made out a report and carried it to the headquarters of General McClellan. He was intensely interested in the news that had been brought him and heartily congratulated the spy on her work. The rifle which she had carried from the Confederate lines was an object of much curiosity, and it is now said to be in one of the museums in the national capitol as a memento of the war.

It was several weeks before the female spy received her second assignment, and then when it came a new disguise was necessary. The African costume was abandoned and she decided to go into the Confederate lines this time in the capacity of an Irish apple woman, so she procured the dress and outfit that was necessary for this impersonation and also practiced the brogue that might be needed to carry her through the emergency. The bridges were not finished across the Chickahominy when she was ready to cross the river, so she packed up her new disguise in the cake and pie basket and swam across the river mounted on her horse, which was known as Frank. Reaching the other side she dismounted and led him to the edge of the water. Giving him a farewell pat she permitted him to swim back to the other side, where a soldier awaited his return.

It was night, and as she did not know the precise distance to the enemy's picket lines she thought it best to avoid the road and consequently determined to spend the night in the swamp. It required some time to put on her new disguise and to feel at home in the clothes. She whimsically said at the time that she thought the best place for her début as an apple woman was the Chickahominy swamp. She did not propose this time to pass the enemy's lines in the night, but to present herself at the picket line at a seasonable hour and to ask admission as one of the fugitives of that

section who was flying at the approach of the Yankees.

In crossing the river she had her basket strapped on
her back and did not know that its contents were completely drenched until she was required to use them.
Later she discovered with much terror that she was
suffering from fever and ague as a result of spending
the night in the wet clothing in that malaria infested
region. Her mind began to wander and she became
delirious. There seemed to be the horrors of a thousand deaths centered around her. She was tortured
by fiends of every shape and magnitude, but morning
came at last and she was aroused from the nightmare
which had paralyzed her senses by the roar of the cannon and the screaming of the shells.

The cannonading ceased in a few hours, but the
chills and fever clung to the spy and were her constant
companion for two days and two nights. At the end
of that time she was certainly an object of pity; with
no medicine or food and little strength, she was almost
in a state of starvation. Her pies and cakes were
spoiled and she had no means of procuring more. It
was nine o'clock in the morning of the third day after
crossing the river when she started to what she thought
was the enemy's lines. She traveled from that time
until four o'clock in the afternoon and was then deeper
in the swamp than when she started. As it was a dark
day in every sense of the word, she had neither sun
nor compass to guide her, but at five o'clock the booming of cannon came to her like music, because it was
the signal that would guide her out of the wilderness.

She turned her face in the direction of the scene of action and soon after emerging from the swamp she saw a small white house in the distance.

The house was deserted with the exception of a sick Confederate soldier who lay on a straw tick on the floor in a helpless condition. He had been ill with typhoid fever and was very weak.

He told her, however, that the family who had occupied the house had left some flour and corn meal but did not have time to cook anything for him. This was good news to the exhausted spy, and she soon kindled a fire and in less than fifteen minutes a large hoe cake was in the process of baking. She found some tea packed away in a small basket and the cake being cooked and the tea made she fed the poor famished man as tenderly as if he had been her brother, and after that she tended to the cravings of her own appetite. But it was quite evident that the man could not recover. He was dying. She did everything in her power to make him comfortable, but it was quite plain that he only had a few hours to live. While she stood by his side he said:

"I have a last request to make. If you ever pass through the Confederate camp between this and Richmond inquire for Major McKee of General Ewell's staff and give him a gold watch which you will find in my pocket. He will know what to do with it, and tell him I died happy and peaceful."

His name was Allen Hall. Taking a ring from his finger he tried to put it on hers, but his strength failed and after a pause he said:

"Keep that ring in memory of one whose sufferings you have alleviated and whose soul has been refreshed by your presence in the hour of dissolution."

He folded his hands together as a little child would do at its mother's knee. She gave him some water, raised the window and used her hat for a fan and then sat down, as she put it, "And watched the last glimmering spark of life go out from those beautiful windows of the soul."

He died at twelve o'clock that night and after the involuntary nurse had wrapped the form of her late patient in his winding sheet she laid down in a corner of the room and slept soundly until six o'clock in the morning. It was a curious situation, but it did not seem to affect the nerve of this remarkable woman. She cut a lock of hair from the head of the dead man, took the watch and a small package of letters from his pocket and left the house.

On examining the basket in which she had found the tea she discovered a number of articles which assisted her in assuming a more perfect disguise. There was mustard, pepper, an old pair of green spectacles and a bottle of red ink. Of the mustard she made a strong plaster about the size of a silver dollar and tied it on one side of her face until it blistered thoroughly.

She then removed the blister and put on a large patch of black court plaster. After giving her pale complexion a deep tinge with some ochre which she found in a closet, she put on her green glasses and Irish hat. She had previously made a tour of the house to find the fixings which an Irish woman would be supposed to carry with her in such an emergency, for she fully expected to be searched before she was admitted through the lines.

She followed the Richmond road about five miles before meeting any one. At length she saw a sentinel in the distance, but before he observed her she sat down to rest and prepare her mind for the coming interview. While thus waiting to have her courage reënforced, she took from her basket the black pepper and sprinkled a little of it on her pocket handkerchief, and then applied the moisture to her eyes. The effect of it was all that could be desired, for taking a view of her face in a small mirror which she always carried, she perceived that her eyes had a fine tender expression which added very much to their beauty. She now resumed her journey and displayed a flag of truce, a window curtain which she had brought from the house where she had stopped over night. As she came nearer, the sentinel signaled for her to advance, which she did as fast as she could under the circumstances. He cross questioned her at some length and then permitted her to pass along the road, saying that she might go wherever she pleased.

After thanking the man for his kindness, she went her way toward the Confederate camp. She had not gone far when he called her back and advised her not to stay in the camp over night, adding:

"One of our spies has just come in and reported that the Yankees have finished the bridges across the Chickahominy and intend to attack us either to-day or to-night, but Jackson and Lee are ready for them.

We have masked batteries in all parts of the road. There is one over there that'll give them fits, if they come this way."

This was important information, and Miss Edmonds made up her mind at once that she must get all the news that was possible before night and then make her way back to the Union camp before the battle began. At five o'clock that afternoon she met Major McKee, and, carrying out the promise she made to the dying Confederate, she delivered to him the watch and package. She did not require any black pepper to assist the tears in performing their duty, for the sad mementoes which she had just delivered were a forcible reminder of the scenes of the past night, and she could not refrain from weeping. The major, grave and stern as he was, sat there with his face between his hands and sobbed like a child. Soon he rose to his feet, surveyed her from head to foot and said:

"You are a faithful woman and you shall be rewarded."

At his request she consented to show a detachment of the guards the house where Allen's body lay. They made their way there cautiously, lest they should be surprised by the Federals. Miss Edmonds rode at the head of the little band of Confederates as a guide, not knowing but that she was leading them into the jaws of death. They traveled thus for five miles, silently, thoughtfully and stealthily. The sun had gone down when they came in sight of the little white cottage in the forest where she had so recently spent such a strange night. As they drew near and saw no sign of approaching Federals, they regretted that they had not brought an ambulance, but Miss Edmonds did not regret it for the arrangement suited her admirably. They were soon at the gate of the house. The sergeant ordered the corporal to proceed inside with a squad of men and bring out the corpse while he stationed the remaining men to guard all the approaches to the house. He then asked Miss Edmonds to ride down the road a little way to watch out for the Yankees with instructions to ride back as fast as possible if she detected any of the hated tribe.

She assented joyfully. It was the very thing for which she had been watching and waiting. She turned and rode slowly down the road, but not seeing or hearing anything of the Yankees whimsically thought it best to keep on in that direction until she did. She says that she was like the Zouave after the battle of Bull Run who said he was ordered to retreat but not being ordered to halt in any particular place preferred to keep on until he reached New York. So Miss Edmonds preferred to keep on until she reached the Chickahominy where she reported all the information she had gathered to the Federal general who was in charge.

The news that she brought was of the highest importance and proved to be of great assistance to the officers in arranging their final plans for the forthcoming battle. This was the last feat undertaken by Miss Edmonds, and by a curious chain of circumstances it enabled her to take part in one of the most thrilling battles of the war.

The battle of Hanover Court House is counted among the heroic engagements of that year, and was a very important victory for the army of the Potomac.

Three days after this battle while the army was divided by the Chickahominy River, a portion of the troops having crossed over the day before, a most fearful storm swept over the peninsula accompanied by terrible exhibitions of lightning and explosions of thunder. The water came down in torrents and there were great floods, completely engulfing the valley through which the Chickahominy flows and turning the narrow stream into a broad river as well as converting the swamps into lakes.

On the 30th of May, the enemy, taking advantage of this terrible state of affairs, came rushing down upon the Union troops in immense force. A battle opened at about one o'clock in the afternoon and after three hours of desperate fighting General Casey's division, occupying the first line, was compelled to fall back in considerable disorder upon the second line, causing temporary confusion; but the rapid advance of General Heinselman and General Kearney with their divisions soon checked the Confederates.

The enemy, led by Hill and Longstreet, advanced in great columns with three full lines, and came boldly on like an overwhelming wave, as if determined to crush all opposition by the suddenness and fierceness of the attack. It looked as if the Union troops would be annihilated; indeed, it seemed as if the fragments of the army would be driven into the Chickahominy before it would be possible for reënforcements to

arrive. It was at this most dramatic stage of the
battle that Miss Edmonds became a voluntary orderly
to one of the generals. She has told the story in her
own words, which cannot be improved upon. It furnishes a fine climax to her sensational career in the
army.

"At this time," she says, "I was in military uniform mounted on my horse and acting as orderly for
General Kearney. Several times orderlies had been
sent with messages and dispatches but no reënforcements had yet arrived, and taking a Federal view of
the picture it presented a gloomy appearance. The
General reined in his horse abruptly and taking from
his pocket an envelope he hastily wrote on the back
of it with pencil, ' In the name of God, bring your command to our relief if you have to swim in order to get
here — or we are lost.' Handing it to me he said:

"'Go just as fast as that horse can carry you to
General G, present this with my compliments and
return and report to me.'

"I put poor little ' Reb ' over the road at the very
top of his speed until he was nearly white with foam,
then plunged him into the Chickahominy and swam
across the river. I met one general about one hundred
rods from the river, making the best of his way towards the bridge. Engineers were at once set to work
strengthening the crazy structure, which was swaying
to and fro with the rush of the tide. The eager,
excited troops dashed into the water waist deep, and
getting upon the floating planks went pouring over in
massive columns. I preferred to swim my horse back

again rather than risk myself upon such a bridge, for I looked every moment to see it give way and engulf the whole division in the turbid waters of the swollen creek. However, all reached the other side in safety and started along the flooded road on the double quick. This was cheering news to carry back to the General, so I started again through the field in order to claim the reward of ' Him who bringeth good tidings.'

" I found the General in the thickest of the fight, encouraging his men and shouting his orders distinctly above the roar and din of battle. Riding up to him and touching my hat I reported:

" ' Just returned, sir. General G with his command will be here immediately.'

" It was too good to keep to himself, so he turned to his men and shouted at the top of his voice:

" ' Reënforcements! Reënforcements!'

" Then, swinging his hat in the air, he perfectly electrified the whole line as far as his voice could reach and the glorious word ' Reënforcements,' was passed along until that almost exhausted line was re-animated and inspired with new hopes, which led it to ultimate victory."

XVI

THE AMAZING ADVENTURE OF
BRIGADIER-GENERAL
LAFAYETTE C. BAKER

BRIGADIER-GENERAL LAFAYETTE C. BAKER

XVI

THE AMAZING ADVENTURE OF
BRIGADIER-GENERAL
LAFAYETTE C. BAKER

IN the early part of April, 1861, a tall, well-built man, with the love of adventure in his heart, called upon the General commanding the Union forces and offered to penetrate the Confederate lines for the purpose of discovering the military secrets of the Southern army.

The volunteer was Lafayette C. Baker, who was to play a most conspicuous part in the Civil War, and the soldier to whom he made his proposal was General Winfield Scott, one of the most distinguished military men in the United States. The interview was epoch-making in its character, and out of it came one of the most amazing adventures in the history of the war.

Washington was filled with all sorts of men on all sorts of missions at that time, and Scott was not disposed to see the young man from the West. The General, with others in power, had his fill of theorists who offered endless suggestions for the conduct of the war, most of which, when tried, proved to be impracticable. But Baker was the sort of an enthusiast who was not to be daunted. He had journeyed to the

National Capital for the purpose of seeing the General and he did not propose to quit until he had accomplished his object. It happened that he was acquainted with Congressman William D. Kelley, a notable member of the House from Philadelphia, and Mr. Kelley, in the kindness of his heart, managed to arrange an interview with General Scott.

The enthusiasm of the man who was willing to risk his life in the cause attracted the attention of the veteran of the Army. Scott had the enviable distinction of having participated in three wars. He rendered distinguished service in the war of 1812, and he was one of the heroes of the Mexican War. Now, as the ranking head of the Army, he was charged with the direction of the Federal forces in the Civil War, although age and increasing infirmities eventually caused him to be shelved in favor of younger men. But in the meantime he was deeply interested in knowing the plans of the Confederates, and he was impressed with the earnestness of Baker.

"You look as if you had the grit and the intelligence for the job," he said, "and I'm going to give you a chance to see what you can do. If you succeed you will be recognized by the Government in a suitable manner."

Baker drew himself up to his full height and there was a flash of fire in his gray eyes as he exclaimed:

"All I ask is this chance — I'll guarantee to make good!"

The General smiled and placed his hand upon the shoulder of the volunteer.

" That's the sort of spirit that wins.   Good-by and good luck to you! "

But before Baker left, Scott had pressed ten twenty-dollar gold pieces into his hands.

" You may need it for expenses," he said with a humorous twinkle in his eyes.

Lafayette Baker now possessed the status of an " unofficial spy."   He was not commissioned and he was unarmed, but he was satisfied that if he were able to carry out his promise he would not fail to receive governmental recognition.   His first move was to contrive some plan that would make his appearance in the camp seem reasonable.   He discarded the notion of a disguise as unnecessary and dangerous.   He finally hit upon the expedient of pretending to be an itinerant photographer.   At that stage of the Civil War picture taking was all the rage and the officers delighted in having themselves photographed in front of their tents, surrounded by their aides.

Baker went to one of the second hand shops in Washington and succeeded in purchasing a camera and a tripod.   The fact that the camera was worn out and unworkable did not disturb him in the least.   The dealer chuckled at the thought of finding a customer who was willing to pay real money for such junk, little thinking that the paraphernalia was precisely suited to the needs of the purchaser.

All of his preparations were completed on the 11th of July, 1861, and on the morning of that day he began his journey, exclaiming as he did so,

" On to Richmond! "

Baker had been given detailed instructions by General Scott and was told to keep his eyes and ears open during the progress of his trip to the Confederate capital. He had been told to learn the locality, strength and character of the Southern troops and to let no opportunity pass for gaining information of the enemy's fortifications. General Scott was especially anxious to get some definite news concerning the famous Black Horse Cavalry, which had become the bane of the Union Commanders.

Baker began his journey in high spirits. The nature of his services, of course, was not known to the Federal troops and as a consequence he was regarded by them with quite as much interest and curiosity as if he had been within the lines of the enemy.

The Federal Army lay before Washington, guarding the frontier, which stretched from a point three miles below Alexandria toward the Potomac. General Heintzelman was the Provost Marshal and was stationed at this point. Passes were not recognized either by the Union or Confederate armies, and Baker knew that he ran the risk of being arrested as a spy either by the Federal or the Confederate sentinels. However, he knew the attempt to get through both these lines was a part of his self-imposed task. When he was four miles out of the city he reached the headquarters of the Second Maine Regiment. His photographic outfit was slung across his back and the Colonel of the regiment invited him to take a view of the camp, including his own tent with the principal officers standing in the foreground. As Baker's apparatus was next to worthless, he knew that it would be folly for him to pretend to take the picture, but he was equal to the occasion. After dining with the Colonel, he suggested that he would like to go to a neighboring hill and take views of the encampment and then return to photograph the headquarters. He was soon in the woods, and eluding the guards pushed forward through the tangled undergrowth in the direction of Richmond. After a while he felt that he had crossed the Federal lines, but at that critical moment he was startled by a loud command:

"Who goes there!"

Baker looked up and saw a sentinel standing with lifted gun upon a knoll just beyond the roadside. There was no opportunity for explanation. The guard marched the volunteer in the direction of the Colonel's headquarters. That officer was sure he had caught a spy and escorted by ten men, Baker was sent back along the railroad, the very way he had started, to General Heintzelman's headquarters. He was presented to the General in language that was more expressive than flattering:

"Here's a dirty spy, General — we found him lurking about our camp and trying to get through the lines."

"You contemptible villain!" exclaimed Heintzelman with an oath, "I've got a notion to stand you against the wall and shoot you through the heart."

Baker, with all his courage, quailed before this fiery denunciation. He was in a predicament. His employment by General Scott was confidential and it might spoil his plan of campaign if he should disclose his identity, but while he was wondering what he should do under the circumstances, General Heintzelman burst forth with another tirade:

"I'll fix you, you rascal!" he exclaimed. "I'll send you to General Scott and I'll wager that he'll teach you a lesson that will last you for the balance of your life."

The captive smiled at this announcement. It fitted in with his own desires so well that he could scarcely conceal his own satisfaction. A guard was placed around him and he was hurried to Washington and into the presence of General Scott. The veteran lifted his eyebrows with surprise and amusement and dismissed the escort.

"Leave this man with me," he said, trying to conceal his smile; "I'll know how to deal with him."

When they were alone the General patted his messenger on the shoulder and said cheerfully:

"This is a complication that I had not anticipated. What are you going to do about it?"

"I'm going to try again," was the prompt reply of Baker, and ten minutes later he was started on his mission for the second time.

Soldiers were arriving in Washington at all hours of the day and night and in an almost unbroken line were marching over a long bridge into Virginia. That night Baker took his position at the end of the bridge and when a regiment came down in considerable disorder he quietly slipped into the ranks, hoping to be borne along with the troops. Unfortunately a lieutenant saw the movement and taking the interloper by the collar put him under guard and sent him back to the rear. He was released with a warning not to repeat the trick.

Another night was spent in Washington, but it was not wholly devoted to sleep. The active mind of the volunteer was busy with new plans and when daylight came he said to himself with the air of a child who is reciting a lesson:

"On to Richmond!"

Before breakfast that morning he had renewed his journey on foot, going through the lower counties of Maryland, toward Fort Tobacco. He traveled thirty-five miles that day and when night came he was so exhausted that he slept like a log. In the morning he gave a negro one of his precious twenty-dollar gold pieces to row him across the river and before noon that day he found himself well within the Confederate lines. The country was wooded and an unfrequented road, whose general direction was toward Richmond, suggested his line of advance into the old dominion. It was a hot day and he was forced to pause frequently to slake his thirst at brooks by the roadside. He had no settled plan of future movements, but trusted to circumstances to steer his course. He was about four miles from the banks of the Potomac when two Confederate soldiers made their appearance and demanded him to give an account of himself. He did so, but his story was evidently discounted, for the soldiers promptly placed him under arrest as a spy. They were friendly guards, however, and ac-

cepted an invitation from their prisoner to indulge in
a glass of ale at a beer shop in one of the townships
through which they passed. One glass, as frequently
happens, led to another, until finally the two soldiers
fell asleep on the step of the beer house and their prisoner went on his way unmolested.

He proceeded along the road toward Manassas
Junction, congratulating himself on his easy escape
when four cavalrymen suddenly came out of the brush
and ordered him to halt. They drew their sabers and
commanded him to surrender. He pretended surprise.

"I'm a law abiding citizen," he exclaimed, "unarmed and on my way to Richmond, where I have
business."

One of the men dismounted and proceeded to search
him and succeeded in finding a number of letters. It
was just the thing that Baker wanted, for two of these
missives were notes of introduction to prominent men
in Richmond. In spite of this, the four soldiers directed Baker to proceed to Brentsville, about ten miles
distant. They rode all the way and kept him on foot
between them. Brentsville was reached about ten
o'clock that night and the prisoner was immediately
taken to the headquarters of General Bonham of South
Carolina, who was in command at that vicinity. The
General, who was in full dress uniform, took a seat
opposite Baker and began to question him.

"Where do you come from and where are you
going?" he asked.

"I come from Washington and I am on my way to
Richmond."

"What do you mean by coming inside of my lines!" he exclaimed.

Baker's face in the language of the movies "registered" intense surprise.

"I'm a loyal and peaceful citizen of the United States, engaged in an honorable and legitimate pursuit. I have business in Richmond and desire to get there at the earliest possible moment."

The Confederate General laughed mirthlessly.

"Well, I'll see that you get there and in quick order. I believe you're a Union spy and I'm going to send you to General Beauregard."

General Bonham handed a sealed letter to a lieutenant who was standing near by and said:

"Put this man in irons and take him to General Beauregard's headquarters."

So at midnight, expostulating all the way, he was compelled to go on foot in the direction of Manassas Junction. When he protested against being compelled to walk such a distance he was told that he had chosen that mode of conveyance and ought not to find fault with it. The party arrived at Manassas Junction at daylight and went at once to General Beauregard's headquarters, which were located at the Wiere House. The prisoner was completely exhausted from his walk and he lay down in front of the house and went to sleep. He awoke at nine o'clock and found himself in charge of a guard, who told him that General Beauregard had expressed a desire to see him.

General Beauregard sat in front of a desk, surrounded by members of his staff. An open letter lay

before him. He pointed to it, frowningly, and said:
"I see that you have been taken inside of our lines.
What explanation have you to make?"

Lafayette Baker had been cross-examined so often
during his brief career as a military spy that he was
becoming used to the ordeal. He had his story by
heart and he proceeded to tell it glibly.

"I am from Washington and I am on my way
to Richmond where I have private business requiring
my attention. I have not intended to violate any
law, regulation or military rule of the Confederate
Army."

The General turned to a member of his staff and
began whispering. The prisoner watched him anxiously. The letters that had been taken from him
named him as Samuel Munson and he realized that it
would not do to forget the appellation. He had assumed that name because he had learned that several
families by the name of Munson belonged in Knoxville, Tennessee, and he had known a son of Judge
Munson during the time he lived in California.
While this thought was running through his mind the
General finished his conversation with his staff officer
and once more turned to the spy.

"So you are going to Richmond, are you?"

The prisoner smiled.

"That was my intention," he replied, "but of course
you are to be the judge in that matter. If it is your
desire, I am willing to return to Washington."

General Beauregard shook his head.

"No," he said, with a slight trace of sarcasm in his

voice. " I prefer that you should go to Richmond. Where do you reside? "

" I have lived in California for the last ten years, but formerly lived in the South in Knoxville, Tennessee."

" How long has it been since you were in Knoxville? "

" Ten or twelve years."

" What is your name? "

" Samuel Munson," replied Baker with cheerful mendacity.

General Beauregard looked at the prisoner intently and then suddenly exclaimed:

" Yes, yes, I know that is the name on the letters that were found in your possession, but I'd like to know what your name was before you became a spy."

If he expected to catch his man unaware, he was disappointed for Baker, looking at him with assumed dignity, said:

" I am no spy."

The General arose from his chair and paced up and down the room several times. Presently he halted and pointing out of the window said:

" Do you see that tree? "

" I do."

" Well, I half believe that you are a spy and if I was sure of it I would hang you on that tree as a warning to all other spies."

Baker looked at him reproachfully and not without a secret feeling of fear. The General called to one of his attendants.

" Orderly," he commanded, " take this man out and put him in the guard house."

Five minutes later the adventurer found himself inside of a log house within a stockade. The discreet use of one of his gold pieces secured him a warm breakfast and later in the day he was permitted to go outside in the care of a guard. The two men were soon on good terms and the guard did not disdain the offer of a drink with his prisoner. Before they returned, Baker had the satisfaction of seeing all the troops in the vicinity of Manassas Junction — including the famous Black Horse Cavalry concerning which General Scott was anxious to obtain information.

The volunteer spy now had important information which would be of great value to General Scott, but he had no means of conveying it to the Union Commander. Indeed, he was kept under lock and key with no means to communicate with the outside world. Perhaps his guards repented having given him so much liberty. If so they did not propose to repeat the mistake. During the long watches of the night he had time to think over his position, and to consider his plans for the future. As a result of this he abandoned all thought of trying to escape — at least at that stage of the adventure. His one desire was to reach Richmond, and thus carry out his original design. But if he were kept confined there would not be much prospect of reaching the Confederate capital. Curiously enough, the thought of being shot as a spy did not enter his thoughts at that time. He was so much engrossed in his mission that he did not think of the risk he was running. All during that night his one thought was:

How shall I get to Richmond?

Just before daylight the answer came in the most abrupt and unexpected manner. One of his guards aroused him, shouting:

" Hey there, wake up and get ready for a journey! You've got to go to Richmond and give an account of yourself to Jeff Davis! "

Baker could have cried with joy. The one thing he most desired had come about without any effort on his part. He cheerfully arose and won the good will of the guard by his seeming docility. He was taken to the station and placed on a freight car, along with some others who were also going to Richmond. Evidently he was regarded as an important prisoner, for he was carefully guarded during every stage of the journey. That trip during the night, over a badly constructed road was a nightmare, long to live in the memory of Lafayette Baker. But the prospect of actually setting foot in the Confederate capital kept him in the best of spirits and enabled him to exchange jests with his captors.

On the arrival in Richmond he expected to be taken to Libby Prison, concerning the horrors of which he had heard a great deal from Union soldiers who had been captured in some of the early skirmishes of the war. But instead of that he was conveyed to a room on the third story of an engine house in the city. His apartment was large and airy, and was all that could be desired. He was treated with great consideration, but was guarded with scrupulous care. Evidently the officers felt that they had no ordinary prisoner in their charge. The cause of this extreme courtesy became evident on the morning of the second day after Baker's arrival in Richmond when he was informed that President Davis desired to interview him. The head of the Confederacy had his headquarters in the Spottswood House whence the Northern spy was escorted. Baker expected to find much formality there, but to his surprise found Mr. Davis in his shirt sleeves and without collar and tie. He was evidently very busy because his desk was filled with papers and there were a number of persons waiting to have a talk with him. He motioned Baker to a seat without looking at him, and continued with some writing with which he was engaged when the prisoner was brought into his room. Presently he turned to the suspect and said abruptly:

"They say your name is Samuel Munson?"

"Yes, sir," replied the cheerful fabricator, "that is my name."

"I understand," said the civil chief of the seceding States, toying with his pen, "that you have been in Washington recently. What can you tell me about conditions there?"

"Not much," was the answer, "except that there is a great deal of excitement and confusion there."

"How many troops do you think there are in Washington and vicinity at the present time?"

"That is a pretty difficult question to answer, but there are probably from 75,000 to 100,000, with more arriving all the while."

Mr. Davis seemed to ponder over this for some time, and then looking his caller in the eye, he said,

"I presume that you know you are suspected of being a spy?"

The look of injured innocence which appeared upon the face of Lafayette Baker would have done credit to a professional actor. Nevertheless he evaded a direct answer by saying:

"No man is safe from accusation in times like the present."

"But what have you to say for yourself?"

"Nothing except that I defy my accusers to prove their charges."

"It seems to me," said Mr. Davis, "that some one said you were a Southern man."

"Yes, sir, I came originally from Knoxville. The members of my family lived there for years, but in recent times I have lived in California."

"Have you any way of proving that?"

The alleged Mr. Munson shrugged his shoulders.

"I am afraid I cannot find any one here to identify me."

The President of the Confederacy smiled a somewhat sarcastic smile.

"Perhaps we may be able to help you out in that respect. There is a Knoxville man in the city and as soon as I am able to locate him I will have you meet him."

This was startling news indeed and it came near shaking the self-assurance of the volunteer spy. But before he had time to make any reply he found himself being escorted out of the room and taken to his place of confinement in the engine house. He was treated as kindly as before, but he realized that the watch upon him was closer than ever. He did some serious thinking that night. As he looked out of the barred windows and up into the unpitying stars he felt that he had reached a real crisis in his life.

One of two things would happen. Either he would escape from his place of confinement, and attempt to reach the North, or he would be shot as a spy. All of the chances seemed to point to his execution on the charge of spying.

But his naturally buoyant disposition came to his aid, and when morning arrived he was taking a more cheerful view of the future. That day he was taken before President Davis and submitted to a further cross-examination. The Chief of the Confederacy appeared to be more anxious to get reliable information concerning the Union forces than to prove that Baker was a spy.

"Who is in command of the Yankees at this time?" he asked.

"General Scott," was the truthful reply.

"Where is he?"

"In Washington."

"Ah, then he is not in charge of the troops?"

"No, sir, I believe that General McDowell is in active command of the forces in the field."

This was correct, and Baker in making the statement felt that he was not giving away any of the secrets of the war. But the information interested the

President and he turned aside and talked with several of his advisers who were in the room. In the meanwhile he made a gesture to indicate that he was through with Mr. Baker, alias Mr. Munson, and the spy was led from the room and once again taken to his prison in the engine house. In spite of his optimistic nature these repeated cross-examinations were beginning to unnerve him. He was afraid that he might be tripped up in some of his answers, and then he felt sure that he would be stood up against a wall and shot. He felt that such a procedure would make him a martyr, but he had a very natural desire to postpone his martyrdom as long as possible.

His real ordeal was to come on the following day. Shortly after breakfast he learned that Mr. Davis desired to see him again. And he learned something else that caused him much perturbation. It was that a Knoxville man had been located in Richmond and that he had been sent for to identify the supposed Mr. Munson. Baker tried hard to screw up his courage for the interview. He was at a loss as to how he should act and talk. It was certain that the man did not know him and in such an event he would be in the position of being condemned as an impostor and a spy. While he was preparing to go over to the Spottswood House he heard one of his captors speak of a Mr. Brock of Knoxville, who had also been summoned to meet the President. Baker grasped at this as a drowning man grabs at a straw. All the way to the hotel he racked his brain in the effort to work out a plan of action. But he could reach no definite con-

clusion.   He would have to be guided entirely by circumstances.   One thing he did do was to refresh his
mind as to certain names and places in Knoxville.
When he reached the headquarters of the Confederate
Government he found Mr. Davis talking with a man in
a frock coat and a slouch hat.   At first he supposed
that this must be Brock, but fortunately he learned
that it was Robert Toombs, and was thereby saved
from making a break that might have caused his un-
doing.   In a moment the President turned to the spy.

"Hello, Munson," he said, "I have sent for a man
who has lived in Knoxville for many years, and he will
be able to tell us if you are the person you claim to be.
Take a seat.   He'll be here in a few minutes."

Baker sat on a chair facing the door and anxiously
waited for the man who was to give the verdict.   The
moments went by on leaden heels.   He could feel the
cold sweat coming out on his brow.   But he had courage and he was resourceful.   Once the door opened
and a messenger came in.   Baker half rose to his feet,
but caught himself in time.   He could not afford to
make a mistake.   The President and Toombs talked
together as if oblivious to his presence.   Presently
Toombs threw himself on a couch in a corner of the
room and Mr. Davis busied himself with some papers
on his desk.   The spy kept his eyes glued upon the
door.   Out of it would walk his doom or his deliver-
ance — he could not tell which.   Suddenly when the
strain was beginning to seem too great for further
endurance, the door was opened and a middle-aged
man entered the room.   He hesitated for a moment

and looked about him inquiringly. Baker felt that he must be the man. He did not hesitate for the fraction of a moment, but jumping up and hurrying toward the newcomer he held out his hand and exclaimed in a tone of great cordiality:

"Why, hello, Brock, how are you, anyhow?"

The surprised visitor did not have time to think. He accepted the proffered hand in a mechanical manner and said slowly:

"You — you are —"

"Sam Munson, of course. Don't you remember me?"

"Judge Munson's son?"

"Certainly — but it's been ten years since we've met. I'm surely glad to see you. How are you, anyhow?"

"I'm right well," said the stampeded one, "and how are you?"

"Well, I haven't been very well, but the sight of you is a cure for sore eyes. They've locked me up on suspicion, and you've just come in the nick of time. They wanted some one to let them know that I was really Sam Munson. How long has it been since you've been in the old town?"

"Two years," said Brock, watching the other man intently.

"Well, it's been ten since I was there, and I'll bet they've had some big changes in that time."

"Rather!"

"By the way," continued Baker, trying to prevent the other from having time to think, "you remember

the Bradleys, don't you?   Well, I heard not long ago
that Sue Bradley had married — married some fellow
from Chattanooga.   She was a mighty fine girl was
Sue, and the fellow that got her got a prize."

Well, to make a long story short the bluff worked
— not like a charm, but with sufficient smoothness to
enable the nervy spy to save his life.   Brock and
Baker had one or two more interviews, and by ransack-
ing his brain for incidents he had learned about the
prominent people of Knoxville he finally persuaded
Brock that he was really Sam Munson.   The visitor
even went so far as to apologize for his seeming inabil-
ity to place his fellow townsman at first sight.

"But you must remember that it has been many
years since you left the old town, Sam.   You've.
changed a lot since then."

"Don't mention it," was the hearty response.   "I'd
have been the same if I had been in your place.   But
you've done me a good turn, and I won't forget it."

There was no doubt of the good turn — if saving
a man from being shot as a spy can be placed in that
category.

As a result of the business Baker was not released,
but he was placed under parole.   This gave him the
right to wander about Richmond at will — the very
privilege he most desired.   If he had planned the thing
in advance it could not have worked out more to his
liking.   He was free to go and come as he pleased,
and he was actually under the patronage and the protection of the Confederate Government!

For two days and two nights he roamed about until

he became as familiar with conditions in Richmond as if he were a resident. He obtained a mass of data concerning military plans and proposed movements, learned where troops were quartered and where fortifications were being erected. Most of this information he carried in his head, but in a few instances he made notes of a character which were intelligible to himself, but which were not likely to be decipherable to any one else. Finally the time came when he knew more than " was good " for himself, from a Confederate point of view. The question was how to get this knowledge to the Federal Government. The fact that he had been before Mr. Davis and was now at liberty made him seem harmless to most of the officers in Richmond. He became personally acquainted with some of them. One was the Provost Marshal, and so, one day, when he asked that official for a pass to permit him to visit Fredericksburg it was granted without any hesitation.

He proceeded to that place without any difficulty. Once or twice he was halted by sentinels, but the production of his pass was all that was needed to permit him to go on his way. On the night of the day he reached Fredericksburg he parted with another of his precious gold pieces to a negro who rowed him across the Rappahannock. He drew a breath of relief when he reached the other side of the stream, and yet he realized that his dangers had only begun. That night he slept in a haystack — slept the sleep of a dog-tired man, if not of the just. When he awoke at dawn he discovered signs of activity in the vicinity of the barn where he had slept and he knew that he was being pursued. He lay very quiet and listened. Voices were shouting and it did not take him long to learn that a squad of Confederate cavalry was on the hunt and that a number of horsemen surrounded the barn.

He shuddered at the thought of the consequences. He had plenty of courage but he did not relish the thought of being caught like a rat in a trap. He had provided himself with a revolver, and he firmly resolved that if he were detected he would not give his life easily. He grasped the weapon, and lay very, very quiet. He was almost afraid to breathe. Presently one of the cavalrymen dismounted and flourishing his sword began a search of the barn. Some of those on the outside were shouting instructions to the searcher, and he responded cheerily. He poked his sword here and there in the hay rick, calling meanwhile on any supposed fugitive to surrender if he did not want to be killed. At one time the point of the sword just grazed Baker's boots. He could have screamed with nervousness, but by a super-human effort he managed to keep perfectly quiet. And by so doing he saved his life, for the officer turning to his companions called:

"He ain't here, boys — we might as well move on!"

They rode off, to the great joy of the hidden man. He remained still until the sound of the horses' hoofs had died out in the distance, and then he crept from his place of concealment more dead than alive. He waited for a long while and then crept out of the barn and made for the woods. How long he straggled through the woods he could not tell, but he was so hungry, and faint and footsore that nothing seemed to make any difference. That night he managed to get supper in a hut owned by a poor colored man, and afterwards tried to find just where the Potomac was located. When he reached that stream he discovered an old row boat. The owner of it was lying, half asleep, on the banks of the river. Baker invited him to sell the boat, offering the last of his gold pieces for craft, but the owner indignantly refused saying that he would not part with it for any price.

This was discouraging, and in lieu of anything better to do he lay down and went to sleep, with the hard earth for a couch, and the shining stars for his covering. He awakened just before daylight with every bone in his body aching, and an intense yearning for home. The owner of the boat was still asleep, and his craft lay anchored in the water. It did not take Baker long to come to a decision. At that stage of his career larceny seemed a very petty offense. He crept down to the water side and climbing into the boat began to row gently into the stream. The job was not an easy one because the oars were broken and decayed. However, by great care he managed to get the boat into the middle of the stream. At that moment the owner awoke, and when he discovered what had happened sent up a series of ear-splitting screams.

"Come back with that boat, you thief," he yelled, "or I'll kill you."

Baker did not fear anything from the man, but in a few moments he saw that three or four soldiers had

suddenly appeared upon the scene, and were talking
with the distracted owner of the boat. They grasped
the situation at a glance, and ordered him to halt at
the risk of his life. Instead of halting he pulled
harder than ever. Without another word one of the
soldiers raised his gun and fired. The shot struck one
of the oars and shattered it. Once again came the
command to halt and once again the fleeing man renewed his efforts as best he could with the broken oar.
This time three of the soldiers aimed at the man in
the boat. There was a hissing sound, Baker ducked
and the bullets went skimming across the water. The
situation was becoming perilous. The fugitive plied
his one good oar, and worked the stump of the other
with great vigor, and in this way managed to lengthen
the distance between himself and the shore. A final
volley came from the soldiers and this time the shots
fell short of the mark by several yards.

Baker breathed freely for the first time since he
had boarded the boat. He was out of danger for the
time being. All depended now upon his ability to get
to the Maryland side of the stream. It was a hard
job, but he stuck at it with the persistence of a desperate man, and eventually felt the small craft grazing
the beach. He felt a strong desire to cheer, but he
overestimated his strength, for the moment he climbed
out of the boat he fell to the ground, exhausted. The
perils and the privations he had undergone were
enough to kill a less resolute and less hardy man. He
lay on the shore for more than an hour, until finally
a farmer passing that way halted and picked him up.

He was taken to a farmhouse, and given a meal which he ate with the ravenousness of a wolf. His hosts were naturally filled with curiosity, but he felt that discretion was the part of wisdom and he declined to reveal his identity, or the cause of the plight in which he had been found.

That night, in spite of the protests of the farmer, he resumed his journey to Washington. He walked the greater part of the night and slept in a barn as usual. He begged his breakfast and then started on his last lap to the National Capital. It was some time before he felt that he was out of danger, but finally the dome of the Capitol came into view, and he knew then that he was safe and that his remarkable adventure was to be a success. It was nearly noon, and there was a broiling sun when he finally reached the streets of Washington. He did not wait to eat or to make himself presentable, but headed immediately for the headquarters of General Scott. The attendant at the door repulsed him and said that it would be impossible to see the General at that time. Baker knew that this reception was caused by his disreputable appearance, and once he was sure that Scott was in his room, he pushed the man aside and bolted into the apartment where the head of the army was making his headquarters. The General was seated at a desk and as the strange looking specimen of humanity stood beside him, he said rather gruffly:

"Well, sir, what can I do for you?"

Baker threw out his arms in a gesture of entreaty and said with a wan smile:

" Why, General, don't you know me?"

The veteran rose to his feet and closely scrutinized the speaker, and then he said, with a welcoming smile and outstretched hand:

" Well, by all that's holy, it's Baker!"

He would not let him tell his story then, but insisted upon his taking a hearty dinner and making himself comfortable. After that the adventurous one sat down and gave a detailed account of his exploits from the time he left Washington. He presented a complete report of all he had learned while in Richmond, and furnished him with data concerning the size and movements of the Confederate soldiers. Other members of the staff were called into consultation, and after their talk had been concluded Baker was plied with questions which he had no difficulty in answering. It was dusk before he had talked himself out, and then the General took him by the hand and thanked him for what he had done for the Government.

" You have more than made good," he said, " and I will see that you get the recognition which you deserve."

On the following morning General Scott walked over to the War Department, and when he returned he carried with him a commission which made Lafayette Baker an agent in the secret service of the War Department. From that time until the close of the war he participated actively in the work of both the War and State Departments. He was recognized by President Lincoln and became intimately associated with Secretary Stanton. As the result of all this he was made Provost General and later was promoted to the post of Brigadier-General in the army.

XVII

THE MYSTERIOUS "F" AND THE CAPTURED TROOPERS

THE MYSTERIOUS "F" AND THE
CAPTURED TROOPERS

A FAN, a glove, a whiff of perfume, an unknown female spy, and a troop of captured soldiers, taken unawares, constitute pretty good ingredients for a romance, and yet they have been part of the actual history of more than one war.

During the Civil War the Union troops occupied the territory known as Fairfax Court House for a considerable period. It was in Virginia, and might fairly be said to be "the enemy's country." It was one of those army outposts where the men are called upon to do a great deal of watchful waiting. The Union soldiers and the residents of the community came to know one another pretty well, and in the course of time there came that familiarity which breeds contempt of danger. There were social affairs and the people came and went as they pleased.

General Stoughton was in charge of the small Union force which was in control of the town, and there is nothing in the official reports to indicate that he was remiss in any way. But some of the men began to feel that everything was not as it should be. It was rumored that at least one of the women in the place was supplying information to the enemy. Just who it was could not be determined, but presently the word went around that the mysterious spy was known only by the letter " F."

Mosby's raiders were performing sensational feats in many parts of Virginia at that time, and it was hinted that they were in the vicinity of Fairfax Court House. One day one of the charming Southern girls of the town went out horseback riding with one of the Union officers. It was a delightful trip and the soldier greatly enjoyed the conversation of his companion, who was a cultivated woman, who, while naturally having much love for her own people, insisted that she had no feeling against the " Yankees." During the return home she became separated from him, and when he rejoined her, found that she was talking to a man by the roadside, in civilian attire. Not much was thought of the incident at the time, but later it was reported that the stranger was not only connected with the Confederate Army, but was actually on the staff of the famous Mosby.

The house occupied by General Stoughton at Fairfax Court House was one of those Southern mansions which are so familiar in Virginia. It was of brick, with a porch, and covered with creeping vines which gave it a most picturesque appearance. The halls were wide and the rooms large and airy. It is not hard to imagine that the ample drawing-room must have been the scene of many festivities in ante-bellum days. In a word, it was just the sort of setting that was necessary for the remarkable adventure in which

a girl, a famous scout and a captured general were to
be the central figures.

One day a young Union officer entered the drawing-
room of this house, and looking about him discovered
a fan and a pair of gloves upon the large center table.
There was the scent of a faint perfume in the apartment and following it he came across a beautiful girl
to whom the articles belonged. He returned them
with a gallantry which it might be supposed was foreign to a Northerner, but which as a matter of fact
was quite as common as it was in those living south
of Mason and Dixon's line. He was fascinated with
the girl and she betrayed just enough interest in him
to make him want to dance attendance upon her. His
duties were not particularly trying at that time and
as a consequence he managed to spend a great deal
of his time in her company.

Her name — well, he heard it, but it did not make
much of an impression upon his mind. It is enough
to say that from that time the war seemed to be of
secondary importance compared to the ardent affection
he felt for the young woman. They walked together
and they talked together and he lived in a Paradise of
his own making, none the less attractive because it
happened to be a Fool's Paradise. Even after the incident which caused such a stir at the time, he defended
her from the charge of deceit, so far as he was concerned. But it is very evident that information concerning the conditions about the outpost began to filter
into the Confederate lines. Through some mysterious agency all of the details concerning the topography

of the camp found its way to General Stuart, the
Confederate cavalry leader, and then one evening the
thing happened which caused consternation in the
North, and was received with joy and laughter in the
South.

Mosby, the Confederate Guerrilla, from time to
time, obtained information concerning the outpost at
Fairfax Court House, and he finally determined to
raid it in the hope of making some sensational cap-
tures. His little band, which had been recruited from
Stuart's Cavalry, was eager for the venture, and held
themselves in readiness for the order from their chief.
Mosby, who had the loyalty of his men in an intense
degree, was one of the remarkable men of the Civil
War. He weighed only one hundred and twenty-five
pounds and was about five feet, eight inches in height.
His face was clean cut and smooth shaven and he had
straight, firm lips and a nose that has been described as
resembling an eagle's beak. He was just the type of
man who might be expected to engage in dangerous
adventure without the thought of the consequences.

The affair took place on the eighth of March, 1863.
Mosby had been with his Rangers only a month, but
already he was gaining a name for himself in all parts
of the country. Fairfax Court House at this time
was surrounded by large numbers of Union soldiers.
Centreville, only a few miles away, contained a brigade of trained men. Still another brigade of mixed
troops was located on the pike, near the town. This
would seem to be pretty dangerous territory for a
small body of raiders, but Mosby had not been receiv-

ing information for days without understanding the
situation fully. He knew that there was one weak
link in the chain of defenses and he knew precisely
where to look for it. He proceeded in the direction
of this weak spot, followed by twenty-nine of his
most daring men. It was pitch dark and impossible
to see more than a few feet ahead. Presently they
found themselves in the Court House Square, in the
center of the town. A picket coming out of the darkness called out:

"Who goes there?"

"A friend," came the reply in a muffled voice.

"Advance and give the countersign," came from
the sentinel.

Two of Mosby's men did advance, but they did not
give the countersign. On the contrary they threw
a coat about the man's head, and before he realized
what was going on he had been tied and gagged, and
placed near the roadside where he was not likely to do
any damage to the expedition. The men were now
given specific directions by Mosby as to their duties.
The proof that he had been in receipt of confidential
messages from the outpost was shown by the fact that
he was able to direct each of the men to the particular place where he would find a particular Union officer. They separated and went in squads to different
parts of the city. Mosby was particularly anxious to
capture Colonel Wyndham, because that officer had sent
him a fantalizing message only a few days before; but
when he arrived at Wyndham's tent he discovered
that his man was not there. As a matter of fact the

officer had been summoned to Washington only that
morning and thus escaped the humiliation of being
captured by Mosby.

In the meanwhile, as his officers went about their
various assignments, the chief raider made for the
headquarters of General Stoughton. The large front
door was unlocked, of course, and Mosby proceeded
upstairs to the room which he knew was occupied by
the Union officer. He tapped at the door and in a
little while it was opened by a young lieutenant who
was only partly dressed. He rubbed his eyes and
demanded to know the cause of such a visit at such an
unearthly hour. Mosby, who seemed to be enjoying
the situation, took him to one side and ordered him to
take care not to speak loudly or he would shoot him
instantly. He demanded to be taken to the bedside of
General Stoughton, and as the young man was
unarmed, and startled into the bargain, he complied
with the request. Once by the bedside the Guerrilla
Chieftain gave the sleeping man a terrific whack that
awakened him and brought him out of bed in a hurry.
He was furious, but before he could say a word the
invader said in a tragic whisper:

"Did you ever hear of John S. Mosby?"

"Certainly," was the quick rejoinder. "Have you
captured him?"

"No," was the laughing reply, "but he has captured
you."

It was humiliating, but General Stoughton was
unarmed and perfectly helpless. He was compelled
to dress and to go with his captor, who by this time

was reënforced by a number of his men. They went in the direction of the Court House Square where they found the remainder of the raiders, with a large number of prisoners lined up and ready for departure. There were in all, fifty or sixty prisoners and fifty-eight horses. In the darkness some of the prisoners escaped. As the party passed a dwelling in the town a voice from an upper window demanded to know who they were. It happened to be the Lieutenant-Colonel of a New York Regiment. Two of Mosby's men were sent into the house to add him to the prizes already in hand but he managed to elude them and to escape.

But how did Mosby and his men get out of Fairfax Court House without arousing the soldiers in the vicinity? Let that be told by Mr. John W. Munson, who was one of the famous raiders, and who has written a most entertaining story of their exploits. " It was always Mosby's care," he says, " to get his men out of the troubles into which he led them. The troops in the town knew of his presence, but each man of them seemed to be looking out for himself, and there was no concert of action. Mosby started toward Fairfax Station to throw his pursuers off their guard, and then suddenly turned toward Centreville. 'To pass that point meant a great deal to him. The heavy guns looked down frowningly on him only a few hundred yards away, and the sentinels on the works with ' Who goes there?' hailed him as he passed under them, but he made 'no' reply. Silently the little troop passed along by the big guns of the forts with their prisoners

and vanished into the darkness. Captain Barker, one
of the prisoners, made a dash toward the fort but was
shot at by one of the guerrillas and recaptured just as
his horse fell into a ditch.

"One more serious danger confronted Mosby.
Cub Run, just beyond Centreville, was overflowing.
. Back of the little band of raiders was the fort with its
brigade of soldiers, soon to be, if not already alarmed;
in front of them a raging torrent. There was not an
instant of hesitation but, plunging into the mad stream,
the whole party swam safely across, although many
were carried downstream with the current. Once on
the other side pursuit seemed almost impossible and,
as the sun rose above the eastern horizon, Mosby
breathed his first sigh of relief. Even at that hour he
knew that he had graven his name in history never to
be effaced. He had performed another feat entirely
new in the annals of war, and one that was never to be
repeated. In time he reached Culpepper Court House
and turned his prisoners over to General Fitz Hugh
Lee, who was a classmate of General Stoughton's at
West Point."

In the morning Lieutenant-Colonel Johnston started
in pursuit of Mosby, but it was too late to capture him
or to save the prisoners who had been caught so cleverly. The news spread to all parts of the country and
was given an importance far beyond its military meaning. It was humiliating, of course, but it did not have
any positive effect upon the remaining days of the war.
The most interesting comment, as might be expected,
came from President Lincoln, who, when informed

that one of his generals and a large number of horses
had been captured said, dryly:

"I'm sorry about the horses. I can make Briga-
dier-Generals easily, but I can't make horses."

But the Confederates were not disposed to look upon
the matter so lightly. They knew the value of such
an exploit in stirring up the enthusiasm of the people,
and Mosby was advertised as a popular hero. General
Stuart went so far as to issue a special order proclaim-
ing the incident. It read as follows:

"Captain John S. Mosby has for a long time
attracted the attention of his generals by his
boldness, skill and success, so signally displayed
in his numerous forays upon the invaders of his
native State.

None know his daring enterprise and dashing heroism better than these foul invaders
though strangers themselves to such noble
traits.

His late brilliant exploit, the capture of General
Stoughton, U. S. A., two captains, thirty other
prisoners, together with their arms, equipments
and fifty-eight horses, justifies this recognition
in General Orders. The feat, almost unparalleled
in the war, was performed in the midst of the
enemy's troops, at Fairfax Court House, without
loss to Virginia.

The gallant band of Captain Mosby share the
glory as they did the danger of this enterprise,
and are worthy of such a leader."

Secretary of War Stanton was very angry over the
incident. He felt that it was the result of bad man-
agement in permitting Union secrets to be discovered
by the enemy and he was determined to know just
how it had happened. Secretary Stanton sent for
General Lafayette C. Baker, then Chief of the Federal
Secret Service, and instructed him to make a thorough
investigation and to make any arrests that might be
deemed necessary. Baker had already made a survey
of the grounds at Fairfax Court House, and was
familiar with the incidents of the raid. He was perfectly satisfied that the Union soldiers had been
betrayed by a spy. And he came to another important conclusion.

It was that the work had been done by a woman
spy!

How could he ascertain the identity of the woman
and how could he prove her guilt? These were not
the sort of questions to be easily answered. Baker
suspected the daughter of one of the leading citizens
of Fairfax Court House, but he had too much experience in handling delicate matters of the war to think
of arresting a woman without having proof of her
guilt. It would not do to place the case in the hands
of the soldiers. Their methods were likely to be
crude, and besides might cause complications. He
thought over the matter for some time and then he
made a momentous decision. He decided to place the
case in the hands of a woman operative in his own
office.

It was to be a case of woman against .woman!

The woman operative, who shall have to be known as Miss Clarke, prepared for her part with the greatest care. She even perfected herself in the charming Southern dialect so that she should be immediately taken for a daughter of the Sunny South. It was probably a week after the Mosby raid that a fine-looking and apparently embarrassed woman arrived at Fairfax Court House. Finally she managed to enlist the attention of the young woman who was known all through the transaction as " F." The stranger, with feminine impulsiveness, gave her complete confidence to " F." She said that she was greatly attached to the Confederate cause, that she was really a friend and an agent of the South and that she wanted advice and assistance in an effort to reach Warrington. " F," who was the spy that had betrayed Stoughton to Mosby, literally received the newcomer with open arms. She took her to her own home where she was given a warm reception. Miss Clarke was given a repast which included corn muffins, and when they were placed before her she exclaimed:

" This makes me feel that I am home again in the good old South. It has been terrible to have to live in the North with those Yankees. I have never seen a corn cake since I left the Virginia line."

Everybody laughed at this and everybody was happy. It really seemed like a family reunion. The visitor was petted and patronized and made to feel that she was a person of great importance. And why not? Wasn't she engaged in carrying dispatches to the lead-

ers of the Confederacy — dispatches which might
result in the downfall of the Yankee Government?
They forebore to ask her the nature of the confidential
information which she claimed to be taking to Warrington.   Naturally she would be reluctant to impart
that even to such good friends as they had shown themselves.

How did Miss Clarke feel under these circumstances?   Did she have qualms of conscience at the
thought of eating the bread of the family she might
soon be called upon to denounce?   Not in the least.
She knew that the young woman before her had already betrayed the Union soldiers from a sense of loyalty to her section, and Miss Clarke did not have the
slightest compunction about betraying " F " in turn.
But the thing was to get the proof.   She could give
evidence that the family of " F " sympathized with
the Confederacy and was willing to do anything to aid
them, but that was not sufficient for her purpose.
How could she get evidence — documentary evidence
if possible?

The answer came quicker than she had hoped for.
" F " invited her to her bedroom, and when they had
closed the door said to the visitor,

" I have something I am going to show you.   I think
it will interest you for we are engaged in the same
cause."

With that she reached under the mattress and
brought forth a document which she handed to her
visitor. Miss Clarke read it with glowing eyes. It
ran as follows:

MAJOR-GENERAL J. E. B. STUART

TO ALL WHOM IT MAY CONCERN, KNOW
YE: That reposing special confidence in the patriotism and fidelity of "F," I, James E. B. Stuart, by
virtue of the power vested in me as Brigadier-General
in the provisional army of the Confederate States of
America, do hereby appoint and commission her my
honorary aide-de-camp, to rank as such from this
date.

She will be obeyed, respected and admired by all
lovers of a noble nature.

Given under my hand and seal at the headquarters
Cavalry Brigade at Camp Beverly the Seventh day of
October, A. D., 1861, and the first year of our inde-
pendence.

(Signed) J. E. B. STUART,

By the General: L. TIEMAN,

Assistant Adjutant General.

Here was evidence of a most damaging character.
Miss Clarke could scarcely restrain her emotions at the
important discovery. "F" noticed this and instead
of suspecting that all was not well, took the actions of
her companion as the natural expressions of feeling
under the circumstances. She put a question to the
other:

"Don't you feel frightened sometimes — you are
engaged in very dangerous work."

"I know that very well," replied Miss Clarke, "but
I am sustained by the thought that I am doing it for
the sake of my country."

This was followed by an embrace on the part of the

two women — both spies, but only one conscious of
the true conditions.   It might be supposed that having obtained proof of the identity and the complicity
of " F " that Miss Clarke might go on her way.   But
she remained for twenty-four hours longer and in that
time obtained a mass of information, not only concerning the suspected woman, but also about the location
and the movement of the Southern troops.   Finally
she departed — departed with another kiss and embrace.

Two days later Sergeant Odell, connected with the
staff of General Baker, called at the residence of one
of the leading citizens of Fairfax Court House and
demanded to see his daughter.   The young woman
came into the room.

" What can I do for you? " she asked calmly.

" You have been identified as ' F,' the famous
Southern spy," said the officer, " and I have come here
for the purpose of taking you into custody."

She submitted without a murmur and with a smile.
Evidently she knew the danger of her calling and
expected to be arrested at any time.   The young
woman was searched and in her possession were found
a number of letters and papers from Southern officers.
Also was found her commission from General Stuart
which Miss Clarke had considerately left behind.   At
the time Odell was placing " F " under arrest other
officers were making a search of her home which was
still occupied by members of her family.   They found
quite a number of damaging papers, and also a large
quantity of Confederate money.   That same night

" F " was taken to Washington and lodged in the old
Capital prison.

General Baker, in a report upon the subject which
he made to Edwin M. Stanton, the Secretary of War,
enclosing this commission, said:

" This document, undoubtedly authentic and bearing
the genuine signature and private seal of General J. E.
B. Stuart, is of itself strong evidence of the apprecia-
tion of which ' F's ' treasonable services as a spy and
informer were held by her Rebel employers. The
proof of ' F's ' former employment in the service may
be considered indisputable; that of her more recent
services and especially in connection with the late
attack upon our outpost at Fairfax Court House is
not less conclusive; that proof consists in the voluntary acknowledgment and declaration by ' F ' that she
made herself acquainted while a resident within our
lines at Fairfax Court House of all the particulars
relating to the numbers of our forces there and in the
neighborhood, the location of our camps, the places
where officers' quarters were established, the precise
points where our pickets were stationed, the strength
of the outposts, the names of officers in command, the
nature of general orders and all other information
valuable to the Rebel leaders; that such information
had been communicated by her to Captain Mosby of
the Confederate Army immediately before the attack
on our outposts above mentioned; and that it has been
in consequence of the precision and correctness of
such information that Captain Mosby had been enabled
successfully to attack and surprise the pickets and out-

posts of our forces, to find without delay or difficulty
the quarters of General Stoughton and other United
States officers, to capture that officer and a large
amount of Government property and effect a large
return within the Confederate lines.

"'F' also stated to my informant that Captain
Mosby had, but a short time before the rebel raid at
Fairfax, been a guest at 'F's' house at that place,
that he had remained there three days and three nights,
disguised in citizen's dress and that during such visit
she had given to him all the information and details
which afterward enabled him successfully to attack
our forces. 'F' also stated that on an occasion while
she was taking a ride on horseback, accompanied by a
member of General Stoughton's staff, they were met
by Captain Mosby, also on horseback, but in citizen's
dress and that she and Captain Mosby recognized and
saluted each other."

The official histories of the Civil War are singularly
silent regarding the fate of the celebrated " F." Was
she tried and convicted? Or was she acquitted and
released? Her identity was proven, but it is not written in the records of the war, and consequently it is
not given in this narrative. It is known that President
Lincoln, with his shrewd, common sense, and his wonderful ability to make the best of perplexing situations, did not look upon the girl as a dreadful offender.
But if he was not willing to condemn her, he was not
disposed to formally condone her offense. What happened to her? Can it be possible that the door of her
cell was conveniently left open one night, and that on

the following morning she was not found in her accustomed place? Quite likely. At all events the reader
is free to draw any conclusion he, or she, may like.

One thing certain is that she did return to her home
in Virginia, and that her descendants are to-day among
the residents of the Old Dominion.

XVIII

THE MYSTERIOUS MAN WHO ASKED
FOR A LIGHT

XVIII

THE MYSTERIOUS MAN WHO ASKED
FOR A LIGHT

ONE afternoon in the summer of 1898, a shrewd, bright-eyed looking man stepped up to another man in a corridor of a hotel in Toronto, Canada, and asked him if he would give him a light for his cigarette.

A trivial incident, one might say, and yet upon that insignificant episode rested a movement which had for its object the ridding of the United States of Spanish spies in the war which was then going on between this country and the Kingdom of Spain.

In order to make this veracious record perfectly clear it is necessary to retrace our steps. For many months prior to the time mentioned, the relations between the United States and Spain had been greatly strained because of the troublesome Cuban situation. President McKinley had entered a serious protest to the King of Spain, and told him that it was important for our peace that the Cubans should be pacified. But they were not pacified, and things went on from bad to worse until they came to a startling and dramatic climax on the fifteenth of February, 1898, when the cruiser *Maine* was blown up in the harbor of Havana and a number of Americans were killed.

A wave of indignation swept the country from
Maine to California. A chorus went up from all
classes in favor of demanding satisfaction from Spain
— for, in the popular mind, Spain was responsible for
the outrage. The cry everywhere was " Remember
the *Maine!* " Prior to that time the Spanish Minister
had been recalled from Washington because of an
indiscretion, and now our Minister at Madrid, General
Woodford, was handed his passports, and on April 22,
President McKinley issued a proclamation saying that
a state of war existed between this nation and Spain.

That is history and is known to all. What followed
is likewise history, but it is by no means so well known.
The first act of the State Department was to inform
all of the members of the staff of the Spanish Embassy
— in polite language, of course — that their room was
preferable to their company. This seemed like a matter of form that did not deserve much thought. And
the State Department, having served the required notice, promptly forgot it. But there was one bureau
of the United States Government where it was kept in
mind, and that was the Secret Service Division.

John E. Wilkie was then the Chief of that most
important branch of the Treasury Department, and he
had been voted a modest sum by Congress for the
purpose of keeping the country free from spies.
Heretofore his work had been to keep the nation free
from counterfeiters. In both cases he was dealing
with crafty and elusive enemies. He proceeded to
build up a war organization and he posted his best men
in the large cities of this country and Canada. In his

JOHN E. WILKIE

office he had a large map of the United States, and by the use of steel pins he could tell at a glance just where his operatives were located. Thus he had men acting as the eyes and the ears of the Government in the cities of Montreal, Toronto, New York, Philadelphia, Washington, Newport News, Savannah, Jacksonville, Tampa, Key West, Mobile, New Orleans, Galveston and San Francisco.

Now, when the members of the staff of the Spanish Embassy were told to get out of the country Wilkie determined to make it his business to see that they did get out. To make sure, he furnished them with an escort — an invisible escort — in the person of the operatives of the Secret Service Division. He sus- pected that some of them would be so interested in the . game of war that they might be tempted to remain on this side of the ocean and take part in the game. And his suspicions were perfectly correct. For instance, Ramon Carranza, who had been Naval Attaché at Washington, found it convenient to linger in the city of Toronto. That would have been perfectly proper if he had not been found talking to a person who was far from proper.

And this is where this story really begins — with the episode of the man who asked for a light in the semi-darkened corridor of a Toronto hotel. The op- erative who had been sent to the Canadian city by Chief Wilkie happened to stop at the same hotel as the former Attaché of the Spanish Embassy. By a curious coincidence he happened to get a room directly adjoining the one occupied by Señor Carranza. And, moreover, he happened to see every one that came in or out of that room. Also, he overheard some of the conversation that went on in the apartment. Thus on the afternoon with which we are concerned he saw a man with a hang-dog look go into the room, and from time to time he caught fragments of conversation. One of the things he heard the visitor say was "so I will write to the address you have given me in Montreal." There was · some further talk, which could only be heard indistinctly, but the listener managed to discover that the man who was doing the talking had a surprising knowledge of the conditions at the Brooklyn Navy Yard. Presently the conversation came to an end and the visitor left the room. The listener left his room at the same moment, and he came into contact with the other man in the hallway. As they gained the head of the stairway he turned to the strange talker in the most casual manner and said:

"I beg your pardon, but will you kindly favor me with a light for my cigarette?"

The mysterious stranger halted and courteously complied with the request. And in those few seconds in that dim hallway, by the light of the burning match, the Secret Service operative obtained what he most desired — a view of the other man's face. In that brief period of time the characteristics of the suspect were indelibly stamped upon his memory. The two men parted. The one who had been closeted with the former Naval Attaché of the Spanish Embassy went out into the street and proceeded to a remote part of the city. He went to an obscure hotel and registered

and was given a room. The operative of the Secret
Service followed him and at the first convenient opportunity he scrutinized the hotel register. The name he
found inscribed thereon was " Alexander Cree." His
theory was that it was an assumed name. At all
events he shadowed his man. He watched his every
movement, and soon afterwards he sent a code telegram to John E. Wilkie, the Chief of the Secret Service at Washington.

The scene now shifts to the National Capital. Mr.
Wilkie was still in his office occupied with the duties
which pressed heavily upon a man in charge of an important department, and whose force was scarcely large
enough for the work they were called upon to do day
by day at a most critical stage in the history of the
nation. Shortly before midnight the telegram came
from Toronto. It was given to the code man of the
office and in a short time he had transcribed it. In
plain English it read as follows:

" Young Southerner, Alexander Cree, of Hillsboro,
I think, leaves for Washington to-night. My height
and build, small, dark moustache, black soft felt hat,
black sack coat, black sailor tie, somewhat shabby, evidently served on *Brooklyn,* has intimate knowledge of
Naval matters. Just had long interview with Naval
Attaché. He is to write to Montreal."

This was news with a vengeance. There was great
activity about the offices of the Secret Service Division
that night. Several of the best men who were in the
city were quickly summoned and given a description
of the man who was expected from Canada. It was

almost midnight when Chief Wilkie left for his home, but when he quit the Department to get a few hours' sleep it was with the knowledge that he had made arrangements for giving Mr. Cree a hospitable reception upon his arrival in Washington.

That night every railroad station leading into the Capital was closely guarded by Secret Service men. They carefully scrutinized every passenger who alighted, paying special attention to those who were likely to have come from Canada. It was a big job, but it was performed with thoroughness. Many a passenger that night must have been annoyed at the manner in which he was watched by the alert representatives of the United States Government. But, if they felt any annoyance, they must have realized that they were living in war times and must expect all sorts of queer things. Finally, "Mr. Alexander Cree" arrived, and it is significant of the efficiency of the system that he was immediately spotted by the waiting detectives. The description sent by the operative at Toronto had served them well. They recognized him as easily as if they were in possession of his photograph.

From that moment there was a Secret Service man watching him. When one man was tired another quickly took his place, and, as a consequence, there was not a thing he did, and scarcely a thing he said, that was not known to Chief Wilkie a few hours afterwards. His first move was to get something to eat, which was an entirely natural and by no means an unpatriotic act. But after that he went to the Navy

Department, and apparently wandered about in an aimless manner. But, as a matter of fact, he had a purpose in visiting that place. Just whether some one in the Department was acting in collusion with him was not clearly established. Finally he went to his lodgings on E Street. He occupied a second-story room, and as soon as he reached it he made a light and settled down to work before a desk which could be seen from the street. Evidently a quantity of mail had accumulated during his absence in the Dominion, because he was occupied for some time in opening and reading letters. For hours he remained there silhouetted against the window shade while the Secret Service men on the opposite side of the street observed every move he made.

Thus, while Washington slept, an enemy of the Republic and its defenders engaged in a game that was to have the greatest bearing upon the conduct of the war. It is difficult to decide which was the most amazing, the daring and impudence of the conspirator in thus working under the very dome of the Capitol, or the pertinacity and bull-dog determination of the Secret Service operatives in keeping this man under their constant supervision. It began to look as if he would never go to bed. But presently there was a movement in the room and in a few minutes the dark-complexioned man in the soft hat came out of the house and walked across the street in the direction of a letter box. He opened the lid and slid a long envelope into the aperture. Then he turned and went back to his lodgings. In a little while the light was extin-

guished and then "Alexander Cree" retired to sleep
the sleep — if not of the just at least of the industrious man.

But the Secret Service operatives did not go to
sleep. They were more alert than ever. One man
kept guard over the lodgings of the suspect and the
other remained by the side of the letter box. At daylight he got into communication with Chief Wilkie,
and as a consequence of his report an arrangement
was made with the Postmaster of Washington by
which that particular letter box was opened, and the
particular missive dropped into the box by the man
from Toronto turned over to Chief Wilkie. A short
time later a "council of war" was held in the office
of the Chief of the Secret Service. The object of
interest was the suspected letter. It was in an ordinary white, oblong envelope, and it was addressed to
F. W. Dicken, 1248 Dorchester Street, Montreal, Canada. The address instantly called to mind the report
of the operative in Toronto. He had heard the mysterious stranger say to the Naval Attaché " so I am to
write to the address you have given me in Montreal."
It was evident that they were " getting warm " as the
children say in their games. But when the letter was
opened all need for conjecture was past. The amazing communication read as follows:

" A cipher message has been sent from the Navy
Department to San Francisco directing the Cruiser
Charleston to proceed to Manila with 500 men and
machinery for repairs to Dewey. A long cipher has
been received from Dewey at Department at 3.30

o'clock. They are translating it now. Cannot find
it out yet. Have heard important news respecting
movements of colliers and cruisers. *Newark* at Norfolk Navy Yard; also about the new Holland boat, as
to what they intend to do with her and her destination,
I shall go to Norfolk soon to find important news.
My address will be Norfolk House, Norfolk, Virginia, but shall not go until Tuesday."

This was signed " G. D." and was marked " in
haste." The first move of Chief Wilkie was to make
sure that the man was guarded. His investigations
proved that there was no possibility of " G. D." escap-
ing from Washington. Then he got into communication with the Secretary of War and the Secretary of
the Navy and informed them of the information that
had been intercepted. The immediate effect of this
was to tighten the discipline in each of these Departments. All unauthorized persons were to be kept out
of the building and a strict watch was kept upon all of
the employees. The inference was that some one in
the Navy Department had been co-operating with " G.
D." and that this person had supplied him with information upon his return from Canada.

The question of taking the spy into custody was next
considered. It was decided that this should be done
at once. As it was a matter that technically came under the military power of the Government, Chief Wilkie made application to the War Department, and as a
result of this Captain Saye of the Eighth Artillery,
with a corporal and one other man, was ordered to
report to him for duty. Thus fortified, the head of

the Secret Service Division started for the apartment on E Street. The little procession going from the Treasury Department attracted very little attention, and the passers-by did not realize what was going on. But all of those in the little group understood the importance of their mission so far as the Government was concerned.

It was eleven o'clock at night and when they arrived at the house occupied by " G. D." they discovered a light burning in the second-story room. It was evident that the spy was continuing his habits of industry. The Chief gained admission without any difficulty, and, followed by the others, made for the upper room. The supposed Alexander Cree was sitting at his desk engaged in writing. He seemed surprised at the intrusion, but received his callers politely. Evidently his calling had accustomed him to visits at all hours of the day and night.

" Well, gentlemen," he said, " what can I do for you? "

" To start with," said the spokesman of the invading party, " we would like to have the letter you are writing and all of the documents you have in that desk."

For the first time he showed surprise. He smiled faintly and then rejoined:

" Perhaps you will let me know the cause of this unexpected visit."

" Certainly. We have come to arrest you as a spy! "

Cree turned very white. He steadied himself by resting against the side of a bureau. It was some

moments before he was able to speak, and then mois-
tening his lips with the tip of his tongue he murmured:

" Who are you, and what authority have you got for
talking in this manner? "

" It's no use, young man," was the quick retort, " we
have the goods on you, and if you have any doubt
about it we can show you the letter which you mailed to
Montreal and which has been intercepted by the United
States Government."

The spy looked at the speaker helplessly. His white
face contrasted sharply with his black moustache.
For a moment he swayed uncertainly, and fell to the
floor in a heap. He was a most abject spectacle, and it
was necessary to carry him out of the room. That
night he spent in a cell, facing a charge of treason
against the Government, and wondering what his fate
would be.

A mass of compromising letters and papers were
found in the room. From some of these it was proven
that " G. D." was a naturalized citizen and a former
yeoman on the cruiser *Brooklyn*. What had prompted
him to turn against his own country? Could it have
have been some grievance, real or fancied? Was it
Spanish gold? Chief Wilkie discovered many interesting things among the papers that were found in the
room on E Street. Among them was a slip of paper
which contained what is known as Slater's Code. It
said: " To send add 100; to receive subtract 100."
This was the key to the cipher which he was to employ in sending messages to his employers. The cipher contained thousands of ordinary words arranged

alphabetically and having fixed consecutive numbers
of five figures each.   Why he had not employed it in
the compromising communication to Montreal was
never known.   Possibly over-confidence had made him
careless for the moment.

In the meantime Chief Wilkie had his organization
working overtime. The United States map in his
office containing the little steel pins to indicate the position of his men in different parts of the United States
and Canada was consulted repeatedly during the next
twenty-four hours.   Telegrams in code were sent in
all directions.   As the result another spy was captured
in Tampa, Florida.   By one of the curious freaks of
fate this man was critically ill when he was taken into
custody and died shortly afterwards.   But the greatest activity was in Canada.   It was learned that the
Dorchester Street house had only been leased a few
days before, and that it was intended as the rendezvous of the Spanish spies in Canada.   It was clear
that a private detective agency had been organized in
Canada for the purpose of obtaining information concerning the movements of the American troops.

Another amazing thing that was discovered in connection with this spy system related to the manner in
which these men were to work. They were to join
the United States army and to go with the army of
invasion into Cuba, Porto Rico and the Philippines.
When the opportunity offered they were to permit
themselves to be captured by the Spanish soldiers.
After furnishing all of the information possible to the
enemy they were to return to the American lines and

continue their system of espionage.   All of this was
worked out with the greatest attention to detail.   Each
one of the spies was supplied with a plain gold or silver
ring.   On this was engraved the words " Confienza
Augustine."   That was to be their means of identifica-
tion to the Spanish Generals.   Needless to say, the discovery of the plot nipped that scheme in the bud, and
rendered it useless for the remainder of the war.

But what Chief Wilkie and his associates desired
more than anything else was some evidence to directly
connect the members of the late Spanish Embassy with
the operations of " G. D." and the plot in Canada.   It
came sooner than was expected.   One of the Secret
Service operatives who investigated the Dorchester
Street house found some letters which established this
connection.   One of them was a communication from
Ramon Carranza to Señor Don Jose Gomez Ymas.
It was short and sweet.   It said: " We have had bad
luck for they have captured two of our best spies —
one in Washington and the other in Tampa."

This made it appear that the former Naval Attaché
was quite as indiscreet as the supposed Alexander Cree.
At all events, the evidence in the case was furnished to
Lord Pauncefoote, the English Ambassador to Washington, and, upon his representations, the Canadian
authorities made it their business to deport the entire
Spanish outfit.

Two days later the Chief of the Secret Service
Division went to the jail at the National Capital for
the purpose of interviewing the man who had permitted himself to be made a dupe of the Spanish Govern-

ment.   When the door of the cell was opened a dreadful sight met his eyes:

" G. D.," the chief spy of the Spanish-American war, had hanged himself — a dramatic and horrible climax to one of the most interesting incidents in American history.

XIX

CARL LODY AND SPIES OF THE
WORLD'S GREATEST WAR

XIX

CARL LODY AND SPIES OF THE
WORLD'S GREATEST WAR

THE world's greatest armed conflict which began with Austria's declaration of war against Servia on July 28, 1914, and which has since involved most of the important nations of the earth, has produced hundreds, nay, thousands of spies, but the very secrecy which is so necessary to their work has prevented many of them from looming conspicuously in the public eye.

The grim old Tower of London could tell many a sensational tale if its stone walls had the power of speech. At an early period of the war it was estimated that at least a dozen spies had been executed in the Tower.

That being the case, how many spies were shot without the formality of being brought to the capital for trial? How many were executed after hurried " drum-head " court martials? It is safe to say that hundreds perished and that most of them will go down into history unnamed and unknown, unhonored and unsung.

Every one of the nations at war has utilized spies of one class or another. They were captured within the

lines disguised as women, as war correspondents —
even as priests.   In the very heart of the city of London they were caught masquerading as waiters, as cab
drivers, and even as clerks in establishments, both man-
ufacturing and dispensing munitions of war.

Now and then there were glimpses of these war
tragedies which for reasons of expediency are destined
never to see the light of day.   In spite of the censors
there were fragments of stories teeming with red
blood and human interest, even if not of historic importance.

The censorship on war news was strict, but it did
not begin to compare with that applied to everything
connected with the apprehension, trial and execution of
spies.   As a rule, there was no mention at all of these
tragic affairs, although earlier in the war readers of
the London newspapers might have found in the corner of an inside column two or three lines merely an-
nouncing that another foreign spy had met his doom.
Who can describe the pathos and tragedy lurking
behind those few words of cold type?

One day a squad of soldiers escorted a prisoner into
the grim gates of the Tower.   He had been caught
making tracings of a barracks somewhere, and he was
going to suffer the penalty of espionage — which is
death.   It is true that he was assured of a trial that
day, but he saw inscribed over the entrance to the
Tower, " Abandon hope, all ye who enter here."   One
could see the ashy look on the poor devil's face as he
went through the Traitors' Gate, and one could imagine all of the details of the impending business after he

should be escorted into the Lower Green, where all of the official executions take place.

Women spies were numerous in this war, and as a rule they were more successful at this business than the men. One of them had herself banished as a suspicious character from the German border. This was done in order to deceive the English more easily. At one of the barracks outside of London she soon won a host of admirers among the younger officers. It happened that Kitchener was due about this time on a visit of inspection and the woman determined to exercise her wiles on him. Did she succeed? Let the man who tells the story answer that question.

"One glance at the gaunt figure, rugged face and piercing eyes of the man who had avenged Chinese Gordon robbed her of her assurance. She realized that this man, instead of being a puppet, would be a master. She fled for her life and was never seen again."

Some time after that Felice Schmidt made her appearance at Marseilles in the rôle of an apple seller. She was in that neighborhood for many days and evidently was acquainting herself with the fortifications with a view to informing the Germans of the conditions existing there. She was young and beautiful and spoke French with a fluency that deceived the soldiers and the natives of the town. The French soldiers, with characteristic gallantry, treated her with much consideration. But one day she was found in a secluded spot making a sketch of one of the big guns. This led to an investigation. Incriminating papers were found in her possession. She was tried by the council of war of the Fifteenth Legion, convicted of espionage and put to death at the Lighthouse shooting range.

Whatever feeling the British public have had against Carl Lody as a German spy, they conclude that he went to his death with the courage of a soldier. Since his execution it has been whispered that he had a romance with a young girl in Berlin, and that had he succeeded in returning to Germany, he would have been welcomed with open arms by a rosy-cheeked damsel who loved him for the dangers he had braved. In some ways his case was similar to that of the unfortunate Major Andrè, who was captured as a British spy during the American revolution and condemned to death. On the night before he was executed, Lody spent his time in the Tower writing letters to those nearest and dearest to him. One of these pathetic missives was addressed to his sister and read as follows:

"*My darling*: I have trusted in my God and He has decided. Through many of the dangers of life He has guided me and has always saved me. More than to millions of others He has shown to me the beauties of this world and I may not complain. My hour has struck and I must take my way through the dark valley as many of my good, brave comrades have during this dreadful struggle of nations.

" Where I am going there is no worry and there are no alarms. May my life be judged worthy to be an humble sacrifice on the altar of the Fatherland. The death of a hero on the battlefield is perhaps more beautiful, but that has not been my lot. I die here in a hostile land, silent and unknown; yet the consciousness that I die in the service of my country makes death easier. I shall die as an officer, not a spy."

It is estimated that nearly one hundred persons have been tried for espionage in Belgium alone and that at least thirty of these have been put to death by the Germans. The list includes a former burgomaster of Hisselt. The spirit of the Belgians, in spite of their trying position, has amazed friend and foe alike.

The story of a young woman who tried to serve her country and the Allies reads like the pages of an old romance. She managed to get a passport from a German officer giving her the right to leave Belgium, but before going she got into the German camp and became possessed of some valuable information relating to the future movements of the army. This was sketched on thin paper, placed inside the lining of her hat. Her whole aim now was to get out of Belgium without being searched.

She secured a conveyance and started for the border. At intervals of every few miles she was halted and searched.

But as her passport was a letter of recommendation, these searches were fortunately of a perfunctory character. At last she reached the point where it was needful to pass only one more sentinel. As she approached this point, near the border, she heard the order:

" Halt — who goes there? "

The vehicle was stopped and the sentinel, after looking at her papers, made the customary search. It revealed nothing of a forbidding nature. She was congratulating herself that all was well when the wife of a German officer advanced and asked the sentinel:

" Have you looked in the lining of her hat? "

The girl's heart fell, as well it might. The sentinel made a second search and found the incriminating document. She was tried, convicted and shot as a spy.

Another tale relates to a German spy who actually enlisted with a Scottish regiment in France. He was blonde and looked like a native of Scotland. Indeed, there was no trace of German accent in his conversation. He must have lived in Scotland for some years as he had an astonishing amount of information concerning that country. Some of his fellow soldiers insisted that he even had a bit of burr on his tongue, so much did his conversation resemble that of a real Scot. At all events, he is said to have gained command of a company of Scotch Fusiliers. He gave the order to charge and led his men into a trap. Whether he tried to escape is not known, but, at all events, the ruse was discovered and an investigation made. The result satisfied the authorities that a spy was in their midst, and under orders from the colonel of the regiment this pretended Scot was taken out and shot.

Another case that has caused no end of discussion concerns a woman known as Fanny La Place. It was said at one time that she was German and her case has been compared with that of Edith Cavell, the British nurse who was put to death at Brussels. But this parallel is denied strenuously by the French, who give out a statement to the contrary. According to this information, her right name was Felice Pfast. She was a French woman born at Nancy in 1890. She went to Metz in 1914 and later received permission to visit her mother in Belgium. While there, it is said, a German official proposed that she gather military information in Paris. She spent three weeks in Paris and then reported the results to Germans, who, she admitted, paid her 5,000 francs to undertake another mission. She was caught in the act of spying at Marseilles and admitted she had been commissioned to gather military information. On July 10 she was unanimously condemned to death by a court-martial.

Another alleged spy in the great war was Captain Otto Feinat of the Russian army. He was well known in Ruman and was in charge of the judicial proceedings following the Jewish massacres at Kishineff in 1903. He held responsible military positions after that, but it was lately claimed that he had been in some compromising correspondence with some friends in Germany. The evidence against him was circumstantial. He protested from the outset that he was loyal to Russia, but in spite of this he was condemned and sent to Siberia for a long term of penal servitude.

Was he guilty? Who can tell? He had the consolation— maybe a poor consolation — of knowing that scores of other Russian officers have lately been sent into banishment on circumstantial evidence.

Then there is the remarkable story of Colonel Miassoyedorff, who was attached to the staff of the Russian Tenth army corps in East Prussia. The Tenth was one of those that met with disastrous defeat in the Mazuirian lake district. It was under the command of General Rennykampf, and in one of these defeats lost 70,000 prisoners. In a second defeat it lost 50,000. The circumstances in each case were similar. The unexpected arrival of a large force of Germans served to defeat the invaders, and caused them to take to their heels, thus transforming an anticipated victory into a most humiliating rout.

An investigation was started and all of the circumstances pointed in the direction of Miassoyedorff, an interpreter on the staff of the Tenth army. One soldier said that he recognized Miassoyedorff as a man who had been connected at one time with the German army. It was further alleged that at the outbreak of hostilities he had been the head of the German spy system and one of the highest officers of the political police. Charged with these former connections, he denied them most emphatically.

" I deny the charge," he cried, " and I defy my enemies to produce the slightest proof of its truth."

Further charges were made that while he was in command of frontier guards at Verjoblova, only a few miles from the border, he had repeatedly visited the Kaiser and made reports to him. When asked what he had to say to this second charge he merely folded his arms, smiled and said:

" I deny it ! "

But appearances were against him, and after the

WILLIAM J. FLYNN

defeats they had just sustained, the Russians were in a
mood to accept any explanation of their humiliation.
So Colonel Miassoyedorff, in spite of his protestations,
was declared guilty and was executed.

Was he an innocent man, or was he the spy of the
Kaiser?

History may tell us the truth, but history in cases of
this kind is just as apt to be in error as contempora-
neous reports. Such men are unknown, unhonored
and unsung for two reasons. The first is that the
very nature of their profession renders it necessary for
them to lead a dual existence. If they are innocent,
their innocence is rarely proclaimed because it would
be an admission of error. And whoever heard of such
an admission? On the other hand, if they are actually
spies those who care for them most would fain permit
their memory to rest in peace.

The story of the activity of German spies in the
United States would make a book in itself, but it would
be disconnected, fragmentary and unsatisfactory.
There have been any number of unproved charges,
any amount of unfinished stories and countless plots
that never came to a head. But enough has been
proven to indicate that this country has been filled with
spies and special agents of the Kaiser. Chief Flynn,
of the United States Secret Service, with the comparatively small force under his direction, has performed wonders in ferreting out these offenders against
the peace and honor of this country. Scores of arrests have been made and there have been a number of
important convictions. Most of these have been in

connection with the destruction of munition plants, and a few have been violations of our laws in an endeavor to hatch plots against Great Britain and France.

Perhaps the most striking instance of pernicious activity on the part of German representatives was that of Captain Karl Boy-Ed and Captain Franz von Papen, naval and military attachés, respectively, of the German Embassy at Washington. For a long time they were a thorn in the side of the American Government. The President and the Secretary of State were reluctant to act because of their desire to preserve friendly relations with the German nation. Finally, conditions became unbearable, and on the last of October, 1916, the State Department asked for the recall of Boy-Ed and von Papen. It was announced at the time that the action of this Government against the German attachés was due to no single incident in either case, but was based on an accumulation of improper activities connected with the handling of German military and naval matters in this country. It was hinted at the time that one of the strongest reasons for the action was the connection of one of the attachés with a movement to set up a scheme in Mexico detrimental to the interests of the United States.

One can only marvel at the patience of our Government under the circumstances. Captain Boy-Ed's name at the time was prominently mentioned in connection with the Richard Peter Stengel passport case, with the Werner Horn dynamiting case, and with the queer diplomatic fiasco in connection with the case of Dr. Constantine Dumba, the Austrian Ambassador.

Germany informed the United States on December 6, 1916, that she desired to know upon what grounds the State Department asked for the withdrawal of Captains Boy-Ed and von Papen. Secretary Lansing, on the following day, replied that the military and naval activities of the attachés constituted their principal offense, but did not discuss the facts or the sources of information. On December 10, Count von Bernstoff, the German Ambassador, informed Secretary Lansing that the German Emperor had acquiesced in the request of the United States for the withdrawal of the attachés, and before the end of the year both of them had departed for Germany.

Events moved rapidly in the United States after that. On Saturday, February 3, Ambassador Bernstoff was given his passports, and on April 6, 1917, the Congress, upon the recommendation of the President, declared that a state of war existed with Germany. From that day forth the Secret Service, and all of the forces of the Government were used in rounding up and arresting spies and suspects.

Many hundreds of arrests were made by Secret Service agents and other officers of the Government and a score of convictions secured. A large number of suspected persons were interned at Fort Oglethorpe, in Georgia. Probably not one of the arrested persons could be ranked as a great military spy, and yet when all of their activities were pieced together they must have been of great value to the Imperial German Government. The varied character of the work they were doing for the enemy indicated that it must have been

more or less systematized, and that it was in all probability under the direction of some one person acting
as the master spy.

For instance, on the 15th of July, 1917, an alien was
indicted by the Federal Grand Jury, in New Orleans,
on the charge of being a spy. It was learned that the
man had been hovering in the neighborhood of the
local naval station for many days at a time. Once he
was seen to be making notes in a book. At a given
time his rooms were searched, and the authorities
found a number of blue prints and plans of the naval
station in his possession. He was indicted on the
charge of obtaining this information clandestinely
" and for the purpose of supplying it to the enemy, the
Imperial German Government, against the peace and
dignity of the United States." The case attracted
much interest because it was the first time since the
days of reconstruction that any one had been indicted
in New Orleans for a plot against the United States.

About the time of the New Orleans incident a German nobleman was arrested in Toledo, Ohio, for activity in the interest of the Kaiser. The man had made
a sensational escape from Canada, about eighteen
months previously. He had been arrested in Quebec
on a spy charge, and was being taken in an automobile
to St. Thomas, Ontario. Near the outskirts of the
town he attacked the official who was driving the car,
and knocking him into a state of insensibility, escaped.
He took the badge and the revolver of the stricken
man, and made his way to the United States, coming
into this country by way of the Niagara Falls bridge.

He admitted that he had once been a captain in the German army, but denied that he had engaged in any unlawful business in the United States.

In the early days of the participation of the United States in the war, and when the people of this country did not even know of the departure of our war vessels for the other side of the Atlantic, the fact of their departure was published in Berlin, four days before they actually arrived in Queenstown. This was a serious leak, to say the least. The American newspapers scrupulously observed the request of the Secretary of the Navy to avoid publishing the date of the departure or arrival of any vessel. Where did the Berlin authorities obtain their information? That was a question which agitated many persons. It was solved when the Secret Service, early in July, of 1917, arrested three men in New York, for conducting a private postal service, in the interest of Germany. It was claimed that for months they had been sending "mail" to Scandinavian countries for transmission to Germany. These letters were entrusted to the sailors on the ships, and ordered to be handed to certain persons in Norway and Sweden, and by them sent to their destination in the German Capital.

Several bundles of these letters were seized by the representatives of the American Government. It is a significant fact that many of them were in code. They came from all parts of the United States, and from Mexico and South and Central America. The letters were written in English, Spanish and German. Some of them were business communications, and were admittedly harmless. It was proven that this novel " mail service " worked in both directions, letters going to and from Germany. It was also shown that remote parts of Mexico were in wireless communication with Berlin. Significance was also attached to the fact that parts of wireless outfits had been brought in on some of the Scandinavian boats, and that these were afterward erected in Mexico. None of the men were subjected to any pressure on the part of United States officials, and all were told that they had the right to be represented by counsel, if they so desired.

But these arrests in different sections of the country, almost simultaneously, and the varied character of the activity of the men involved, helps to confirm the statement, made on the floor of the Senate, that during and before the war, we had thousands of German spies in the United States.

THE END

CPSIA information can be obtained
at www.ICGtesting.com
Printed in the USA
BVOW06*1830190617
487293BV00005B/12/P